AF292253

A JOURNEY

Growth in Different Levels on Varying Pathways,
Poetry with a Message—
To Show God's Love Throughout the Journey of Life

LAKONYA D. PARSON

WESTBOW
PRESS®
A DIVISION OF THOMAS NELSON
& ZONDERVAN

WestBow Press books may be ordered through booksellers or by contacting:

WestBow Press
A Division of Thomas Nelson & Zondervan
1663 Liberty Drive
Bloomington, IN 47403
www.westbowpress.com
1 (866) 928-1240

Because of the dynamic nature of the Internet, any web addresses or links contained in this book may have changed since publication and may no longer be valid. The views expressed in this work are solely those of the author and do not necessarily reflect the views of the publisher, and the publisher hereby disclaims any responsibility for them.

Any people depicted in stock imagery provided by Getty Images are models, and such images are being used for illustrative purposes only.
Certain stock imagery © Getty Images.

All Scriptural references are taken from the King James version of the Holy Bible. Scriptures marked KJV are taken from the KING JAMES VERSION (KJV): KING JAMES VERSION, public domain.

ISBN: 978-1-9736-6395-9 (sc)
ISBN: 978-1-9736-6394-2 (hc)
ISBN: 978-1-9736-6396-6 (e)

Library of Congress Control Number: 2019906223

Print information available on the last page.

WestBow Press rev. date: 1/22/2020

First and foremost, this book is dedicated to God. Your ultimate sacrifice is the sign of true love. Your love has kept me and guided me. Thank You for choosing me, the quiet, shy girl who never wanted to be the focus of attention. You have taken me on a journey and transformed me to the "not-so-quiet lady" who still doesn't want to be the focus of attention. When I asked, "Why me?" I heard, "Why not you!" Enough said!

I also dedicate this book to my strongest supporters in everything that I do. To my husband, Stacey, I say thank you for always encouraging me and believing in me. I shared a dream, and you declared that I could do it, even when I had to push to believe it myself. Your ability to step out and try new ventures has helped me to step out. Thank you for jumping in full-steam in my pursuit of purpose. I love you immensely!

To my kids, Jaedon and Stacia, you both have inspired me to do my best. You have emboldened me to get out of my shell to do things in order to encourage you to do likewise. There is so much great potential in both of you, along with so many God-given gifts and talents. As my mom did for me, let me encourage you to always do your best. I love you both!

To my mom, Ruby, you first inspired my love for reading and encouraged my writing. As a teen, I wanted a typewriter when a lot of kids my age wanted the latest shoes. You worked extra jobs to buy a typewriter for me, and you also got me the shoes. I've always appreciated and reflected on that effort. I know the sacrifices that you have made, and I will never forget them. Your hard work resulted in a reciprocal need for me to work hard. Thanks for always seeing my potential and pushing my siblings and I to always do our best. I love you.

In Loving Memory—

To my friend Catherine, your words, affirmations, prayers, great friendship, and love emboldened me to take the steps we talked about. Though you were small in physical stature, you were a spiritual giant and a giant of a friend! I love and miss you!

Contents

Preface

I went back and forth over whether to put these poems into book form, into one collection. I kept thinking that there are so many poets out there, so many people who write poems/poetry. At times I felt unworthy, unworthy and incapable of being effective in my attempts at poetry. So I hesitated. I held back. I kept my poetry locked in my heart, even though I know that the purpose of the words contained therein is not just all about me. Even though my pastor has often taught that our purpose is for someone else, I fastened the pages to my heart and proclaimed, "They are not good enough yet."

Then in Bible study one Tuesday night, the subject was Holy Spirit. I received a revelation:

If this poetry reaches **one person,**
Helps **one person,**
Blesses **one person,**
Helps lead **one person to Christ,**
Helps **one person** receive healing,
Helps **one person** feel understood,
Helps **one person** know there is someone who has gone through "it" too,
Helps **one person** keep trying,
Helps **one person** realize that they are not alone,
Helps **one person** feel the love and acceptance of God,
Then this collection, this offering, has accomplished its task.

Letter in Reflection

Fear of failure in "walking out" my purpose has been my ultimate hesitation in writing this work. It is because I have often felt that if my writing does not work or is not successful, I'd be thoroughly empty. Alas, today I caught on to the knowledge that because You gave the gift and desire for writing to me, and Your thoughts are greater than mine in everything, then what You want my gift to accomplish, You will empower to succeed. This is because You have purposed me to do it. I have learned that my purpose is not about me, and ultimately, the crux of it is not carried out by me. I am just the conduit, the vessel, the tool, through which this purpose flows.

My gift may operate differently from the next poet's or writer's gift. My gift may operate differently from the next author's or reader's gift even in the same gift groupings, yet it is still my purpose to deliver my gift and walk out my purpose in the way that God leads me.

God's Love, Goodness, and Sacrifice

God Is Love

We seek love, plain and simple,
To fill a void or emptiness within ourselves.
We are drawn to the need to embrace love.
It's a piece of the puzzle of our makeup
That must have the perfect fit.

We let things, people, and ideas stand in
As the piece that we think is perfect.
Then we jam the warped, ill-fitting piece
Into the puzzle as the placeholder
Where love should exist.

The piece may not fit; it's not a perfect match.
But just because we've found a piece,
We just "let it ride."
We figure that as long as most of the hole, the emptiness, is covered,
We can get enough to meet that need that arises.

But that slot, that empty hole
Was designated, destined, designed
For a perfect piece,
A slot that can't be filled with a compromise.
That piece is love, and that love is God.
And that piece, when properly fit, provides the peace and joy
That we seek.
Because without it,
We are just living a falsehood,
A mirage, a hallucination, a hologram
Of the real, true, authentic, everlasting love that God has for us.

God is the piece
That we must continually seek.
And in our quest to really know all about Him,
That hole gets filled
In its entirety.

Because in getting to know Him,
To know all about Him,
To learn as much as you can,
To seek Him as the lung seeks air,
In this focused, won't-stop, quest,
God's perfect love is revealed
To new levels.
Amped up
In full splendor,
In awe-inspiring magnificence.
And His perfect love erases all emptiness.

The love of God overflows that open slot
And spreads out to all parts of the puzzle.
As it spreads, it consumes, fertilizes, and cements its neighbors,
Causing them to grow and blossom in hope—in love.
Enabling solidarity, oneness, strength,
It sheds light on what was once dark,
And we see with eyes fresh and new.

God's love tramples insecurities.
God's love consumes the fear,
If you let Him,
Knowing that you have God's love,
Walking boldly in it,
Letting His love trample the substituted desires
that became idols in our lives.
Those desires that could cause us to seek them
And to seek things above seeking God.

These things, often masquerading as desires, become fake idols,
Offering temporary love and peace,
But often lead to our own destruction
As we often try to use a stunt double
To imitate a semblance of love.

A counterfeit is a fake
And will not ever be able to do
Or surpass
What the perfectly planned piece was designed to do.
Like anything that isn't real,
It will only serve to temporarily fulfill
The desire we have in our hearts for real love.
Remember—God is love.
He is real.
He is the missing part.

Goodness

Do You know how good You are?
Am I able to tell it?
Words defy my ability to weave them.
An artist's brushstrokes cannot effectively capture it.

Can Your goodness be captured in song?
Can melodies and harmonies relay Your worth?
Can timbrel and harp, or drum and guitar effectively produce
Scales that can measure Your value?

Your goodness surpasses the restraints of time.
Who can tell of Your mighty works?
The numbers cannot catch up with them.
Who can praise You enough?
The heights and lengths of Your goodness cannot be attained.

Do You know how good You are?
Can it be expressed by the capabilities of mere man?
The answer to that is yet unknown to me.
I do know that I'll join with countless others
On a trek to show what that question means to me.

Through me creative ideas flow.
With the work of my hands, I will press hard to show
My rendition of how good I know You to be.

A personal reflection and personal crusade,
A glimpse into a personal plan
To let You and others know how good You are.
I will make it my work to do all that I can.

How Can You?

Lord, how can You bless me
When I mess up?
How can You still speak to me?

How can You pull me into Your loving arms
Right after I stumbled because I didn't listen to You?
I don't feel it physically, but I feel it in my heart.

How can You love up on me
When I didn't love myself,
When I didn't love myself enough to do what's right,
When I didn't love myself enough to stand up for myself?

How can You love me?
I'm thinking it's because You can't help it.
You prove that what they say is true:
You love me because You are love.
You are just love,
And that's how You can.

I'm So Glad

I am so glad that You are not like the world.
If You were like he, then when I sin, You would condemn me.
If You were like he, then when I fail, You would
Ridicule me and make me feel less than.
If You were like he, You would turn Your back on me when I am less than,
      less than what You've called me to be,
      less than what You've poured into me.

I am so glad that You are not like the world.
If You were like she, then when I forget, You would broadcast my shame.
If You were like she, then when I turn a deaf ear,
You wouldn't call my name.
If You were like she, then You would give me the palm of Your hand
      instead of giving me a hand to stand again.

I am so glad that You are unlike the world.
From whom no second chances are offered,
Especially not a third, a fourth, and so on.
From whom comes condemnation and desertion.
From whom there is a pulling down when Thou art a lifter up of my soul,
      helping me to rise in the renewing of my mind,
      helping me to see faith, to really see faith, in that my ascent above,
      tribulations, distress, persecution, famine, nakedness,
      peril, or sword that the world freely offers,
That Your love is a sustaining grace, a sustaining power that
Provides the wind beneath my wings and my sails.
That shelters me from the storm and encompasses all about me
With a protective armor helping me to see the love, to really see
The love that transcends the world's ability to comprehend it.
I am so glad that You are not like this world.

Love Lavished

Love.
Love lavished.
Great love lavished.
How great the type of love lavished,
How great the depth of love lavished,
Smeared on us,
Poured on us,
Overtaking us as waves, cresting.
Heads lifted up—smiling,
Arms open,
Receiving the overflow
Of love.
Love in waves
Powered by love.
The pouring on of love.

Refreshed by love,
Cleansed by love,
Purified by the glistening waters of love.
Shining on the children of God,
Love of Father toward child.
Acceptance,
Completeness,
Security,
Approval—
All needs met.
Always full of joy,
Always full of peace.

Everything I ever needed,
Everything I ever wanted
Bound up and packaged in that love
And given to me as a gift.

Adopted into the worthiness to receive it,
Your love making me worthy of the gift.
Your gift making me worthy of the gift,
Your gift of love lavished.

> Behold, what manner of love the Father hath bestowed upon us,
> that we should be called the sons of God: therefore the world
> knoweth us not, because it knew him not. (1 John 3:1 KJV)

Love of a Hero

Love,
Love written about in fairy tales and romance novels.
Imagine the love that leaps off the pages of great love stories
and into the hearts of the readers.
Love that makes you feel all soft and cocooned
inside the warmth and safety of it.
Cherished, enveloped, and lifted by the love
and the undeniable proof of it.
The heroine seeks these attributes from her hero.

The object of her affection, who will go to all ends of the earth to please
her; He will go out of his way to protect, honor, and secure her happiness.
This hero watches her and rejoices in time spent with her. His day is
special because she spends it with him, truly wanting to know more about
him. He longs to hear of her heart's desires and deliver the best for her.

Who is this masked man? Who is this love-showering romantic?
Who is this steadfast hero?
He is not masked, and He is not hard to find. He is God,
and He patiently waits to give you everything you need.

He is not masked by self-adornment. He is not a mystery.
We place the disguise on Him in our not acknowledging
His call, His query of us, His desire to commune with us,
In not seeking to know Him and learn more about Him.

His desire is to be seen for all that He really is, that
His love be shown and shared with all.
He desires for you to let Him love you so much that no other love will do.
All other false love pales in comparison, coming up as weak
as the fruitless, futile attempts of mere amateurs.

So many perpetrators try to lay claim to Your work, oh, Lord God.
Perpetrators try to falsify a steadfast, enduring,
unquenchable love such as Yours.

The unsustainable meanderings of forces that vainly attempt to
replace You offer no long-lasting satisfaction, no sustainability.
They are imitators, deviously hiding behind disguises. These forces
are really masked, pretending to be You or scheming to replace You.
But they are conditional, emotional, and wanton of themselves.
Their desires are self-motivated and not in resemblance of You.

The source of love from the originator, creator, and founder
of love can't be denied, confused, or replaced.
The love, the greater love, that God gives freely and unconditionally,
The recognition and acceptance of that love,
Magnified in you in your relationship with Him,
In your knowledge of Him and just how much He loves you,
Provides freedom to you, freedom in His love,
His love that cannot be duplicated, erased, or replaced.

Loving This Imperfect Soul

In my frailties, I call out to You.
I know it's my actions that make You feel far removed from me;
My choices that I knowingly made have me feeling unworthy.
How can You smile upon a face as tainted as mine?

Loving this imperfect soul
That yearns for perfection, but sometimes casts off restraints,
That sometimes takes on the selfish man and
Goes by the wayside just to appease self.

It befuddles this mortal mind, overwhelmed by the capacity of Your love.
The breadth and depth of Your love, Your grace, and Your mercy,
That Your love is so vast, Your grace so great
As to forgive my sins, my iniquities as no more,
As You search my heart and see the sincerity
That underlies the words spoken as,
"Please forgive me," and, "I'm sorry," and, "I turn
Away from it and turn toward You,"
As I walk it out, putting actions to my words.

The mortal man does not naturally become so forgiving;
The mortal man would lean toward letting the hurt
Propelled against him have a greater weight.
This mortal man is working on it daily.

But bless Your most holy name that You love this imperfect soul.
That You love me so much that You forgive all my iniquities, and
You redeem my life from destruction
With no condemnation.

Loving this imperfect soul for You is like a
Constant desire for relationship
And for it to be in that perpetually restored state.
You, the crowner of lovingkindness and tender mercies,
See past my imperfections to the heart that clings to You

And pursues You beyond past and future imperfections,
And seeks a cleansing and right walk constantly toward Your perfection.

It is a walk to perfection; perfection is the goal.
It defines the light shining brightly at the end of the tunnel.
It is the warmth to combat the cold,
And the loneliness that seeks to clothe those
Who feel far removed from Your touch.
So although at times perfection for this imperfect soul
Seems so unattainable due to the weakness of this flesh,
I still bless Your name because by Your grace, mercy, forgiveness,
And Your strength, I am able to continue in this walk.
And I am guided and protected by Your ever-present arms around me,
Loving me and holding me, and always picking me up before I fall.

My Heart Speaks

My heart speaks.
Can you hear it?
Can you feel the rhythms of its staccato?
It speaks of need in a dialect unfamiliar to those not in sync with it,
Those who are not in tune with its melody.
The language can only be translated by someone
familiar with the native tongue.
It is not enough to hear the words; phonetics only attest to the sounds.
But can you connect the sounds to form words derived
from the melody as my heart taps its tempo?

Am I going so fast that you miss me?
Do my signals blur past your ability to capture my sounds?
If I slow down, would you glean from me, or would you
grow impatient in the wait to decipher my lingo?
Can you hear what my heart desperately cries out to you?
Should I adjust myself so that you can see
what I feel, that I clearly display?
Do you know what I am trying to say?

My heart speaks.
Can you listen?
Can you connect the words to gather clear thought?
Should I amplify the vibration carried across the airwaves
So that you can know what is there?
So that you can know what is really there when my heart speaks?

Do you care?
Does it interest you enough to invest the time to learn the language,
the language that is spoken from the sounds that my heart beats?

Lessons learned from time invested tend to stay with us.
My heart's song is but my inner beat encapsulated in words.
Can you hear the beat?
Have you heard enough to comprehend?
If you listen, then how much will it take for you to really feel the beat?
The beat of my heart as it cries out urgently to you.

One Way

Way-path-choice
Means-faith—John 3:16.
Method-direction-question: Who are you led by?

One way, one path to heaven, salvation, and eternal life,
    The one and true living God.
One means, by One sent, and One sacrifice—John 3:16.

One love, one gift, one Son for man
    To reap eternal life.

By one truth came redemption, deliverance, and salvation
By the one great I Am,
By one love
From one possessing great wisdom and power.

Three in one, became the One in flesh for us.
The Way, the Truth, and the life: Jesus the Christ.
One gave the order, one carried it out, one exercised the power.
Three in one to provide the One way
To our everlasting Father.

> For God so loved the world, that he gave his only begotten Son, that whosoever believeth in him should not perish, but have everlasting life. (John 3:16 KJV)

> Jesus saith unto him, I am the way, the truth, and the life: no man cometh unto the Father, but by me. (John 14:6 KJV)

Perplexed

Sometimes my heart, my mind tries to comprehend
Just why there are people who cannot see
Just how much love and affection
You have for us.

You show us Your love in countless ways—
       A soft caress of comfort when we are feeling down,
       The delicate whisper of the wind blowing against our cheeks,
       In the beauty and majesty of Your creation.

Your love abounds.
You show Your love in Your desire that all should be saved.
In Your desire for us to make a free-will choice,
To choose righteousness,
To choose right paths and abhor evil.

Your plans for us supersede even our own hopes and dreams.
Your grace and mercy You eagerly give.
Everything about You shouts love and compassion.

I stand, sit, and lay perplexed,
Just trying to fathom why anyone would not love You back.
Why they would not cling to the love that You offer,
       This unconditional gift,
This gift that You give even to those who choose not to believe in You
Or to love You in return.

This gift that is not limited;
This gift that is not segregated.
It is not reserved for only those who believe in
You and the sacrifice of Your only Son,
The awesome sacrifice for the remission of all our sins
That we may have eternal life
And an abundant life while earth is our home.

Even when we have committed sin
And may have allowed condemnation from the enemy to beat us down,
Your love radiates from the core,
The core of the One true source.

And so we can know we are not bound,
But we have the ability, through true repentance, to be renewed.
It's a heart thing!
You hold the code to decipher it,
To know the heart,
To crack the code within you, that indicates whether what you've presented
Is fact or fiction,
To see the revelation of heart matters.
It's a heart thing!

This gift provides an ability to refuel us
As the ones the enemy hopes to proclaim as guilty, alas, condemned.
Yet You, in Your love, refuel us with Your right and steadfast Spirit,
With Your fire!

So why not choose love?
Why not choose happiness, peace, joy, and a sound mind?
The list is unending, outlining the benefits from God's love,
But choose not only for the benefits.
Choose love because God is love.
       And love doesn't end or fade or suffer
       When love stems from God.

Make the choice,
And stand with me to be perplexed,
But not perplexed as in a worrying state.
Stand as in having the desire to let others see clearly
The immeasurable love of God that we embrace.
The reason we pondered on a question
that is unfathomable in our eyes,
Of why we questioned in this why to begin with.
            Why not choose love?

The Dimensions of My Search

What must I do to meet your acceptance?
Why do I have to fit your mold?

The dimensions of my search, part 1.
You say you love me.
Then you neglect me.
I play all your games,
And then you change all the rules.

I do what you say,
And then you condemn me.
Sometimes I feel so alone, yet I'm all caught up.
And what I once knew to be right
I know that I've often ignored and turned away from
Just to be among your throng.

You have deceived me; I see that now.
So what must I do to shake you off,
To cleanse you from my life,
To purge you now that I see that you are against me
And have been all my life?

I'll seek another to fill my void.
I can't be with you, or I *will* be destroyed.
You only seek to use me up,
And when you are done, your lie is that I'll eventually be set free.
But in reality, hell is where I'll be for eternity
If I keep clinging to you and believing what you say.

What must I do?
Whom do I seek?
Whom do I listen to?
Whom do I need?

Someone is knocking at the door.
Who will it be?
Help me make my decision.
I face a dilemma.
What will I open the door for?
Who will be at this door?

The dimensions of my search, part 2.
He spends His time with me.
He waits on me to change, to acknowledge Him.
He knocks, and do I say, "Enter,"
Or do I turn my back and walk away?

He says He loves me, and He means it!
He shows it.
He never wears a disguise.
He doesn't hide behind lies; He'll never lie.
But He is always there for me to love and to care for me.
He is with me at all times.
And He really, really wants to be with me!

I look to the Father.
He is always there.
He is the only One who is always there
To love me unconditionally.

I seek His comfort.
He will oblige.
I seek His friendship.
He's by my side.
I look to the Father.

I'm free to be me,
The me that He created me to be.
I feel so safe; I am secure,
Secure in His love for me.

My search is forever over.
I can now say that when I need a friend
Or someone to lead the way,
I've already received it.
I'll call on love, the love of the Father.
I will trust in the Father.

I am special to Him.
I am perfect through Him,
And I have no need to look for love.
I am never without love.
Whenever I feel or think I am in need of love,
          I look to the Father.

What Leads You to Believe?

What leads you to believe that you don't deserve love
       When God sent His Son to die for you out of love?
       When God told you and showed you that love is who He is?
       When He instructed you to give it
       As in His commandment?
       If He orders us to love our neighbors,
       Then naturally your neighbor should love you.
       So God is supplying what you need, what
       you deserve, and that is love.

What leads you to believe that you don't deserve love
       When you look over a horizon
       Tinted with waves of orange and purple,
       As the sun sets over the horizon
       Or across rolling hills of lush green,
       Carpeting hills stretching as far as the eye can see,
       As a cool breeze beckons you to enjoy it,
       To simply enjoy it,
       How can that not be love demonstrated and beckoning you?

What leads you to believe that you don't deserve love
       When the pure words of a child
       Causes laughter in your heart?
       When the innocence of a newborn babe
       Urges you to love and protect it?
       When the miracle of birth itself inspires you to awe,
       And the glance filled with trust from the baby
       Floods you with warmth?

Think about it.
Meditate on it.
Really take the time to digest it for what it really is,
To get to the bottom of it,

Examining the facts that have been presented
That defy logic; the words and the imagery
That seemingly denies your entitlement.

Fact 1—God is love,
And He loves you.
He simply loves you.
He cannot, not love you.
Love is He, and He is love.

Fact 2—God freely gives grace and mercy, unmerited favor to you
Fresh each day because He knew you would need it.
It is out of love that He supplies it.

See, God loves you past your mistakes—past, present, or future,
He took care to write that in the contract so
That you would know that you are covered,
And the deal is signed, that the love He has is binding.
It is everlasting; its seal can't be broken or erased.
He loves you regardless, in spite of, because of, instead of.
He loves you.

It's a fact that I didn't earn it; you didn't earn this love,
This grace that you can't work for.
Working for His love is not a requirement.
    You don't have to be pretty enough,
        Smart enough,
        Strong enough,
        Successful enough,
        Tall or short enough,
        Skinny or large enough,
        Popular enough,
        Perfect enough.
    It's because His love is enough!

It is a fact that He made you, you,
Just the way you are,
Freckles or without freckles,
Dark-skinned or light-skinned,
Overachiever or yet again trying to find yourself.

He made you.
Everything that He loves about you is in you.
He made it in you.
He loves how He molded you,
How He chose every aspect of you
As varied as the beauty of flowers, the beauty of colors.
As varied as the different species on earth,
Some known, some unknown—varied,
Different on purpose, by design.
But God loves His work, and He loves His work in you!

He loves that you are different.
You are not a carbon copy of anything or anyone but Himself.
He put the best in you, the best stuff, the right stuff, His stuff!
You are the best you that He could have ever created,
And He loves that about you!

God loves you beyond,
Beyond what you feel about yourself,
Beyond what you feel others feel, think, or say about you,
Beyond what your circumstances speak to you,
Beyond your weaknesses or strengths,
Beyond where you come from,
Beyond what you see yourself as or
Where you think you should be,
Whether you are bold as a lion or quiet as a mouse,
Whether you are an extrovert or an introvert,
Whether the world applauds you, glorifying
you and singing your praises.
Or whether you hide back in the shadows,
Longing to be noticed or to be heard.

God loves you.
So what leads you to believe that you don't deserve love?
Believe it or not, that is your choice, but to not believe in His love
Is a belief that is not grounded in truth.

God loves you,
And the fact remains and always will be
That God always loves you, and out of love,
He will never leave you alone.

Witness of Invisible Truth

They say You are invisible,
But You show Yourself clearly, loudly, softly, gently, and urgently.
I feel Your presence around me, within me.
We are intertwined, emmeshed together in the root of salvation.
I am a marionette in Your
production.
I choose that role.
I realize that Your lead is better than any lead
my feeble attempts could muster.
You bring me safely home to harbor when I've drifted astray.
I am led by truth.
You guide me down right paths, beyond stumbling
blocks, past the blackened mire of darkness that, at
times, has cloaked the periphery of my walk;
It is constantly trying to get in.
Darkness can't withstand You; it can't overpower the light of truth.
You, truth, are there in my happiest of times.
You brought me comfort in my saddest of times.
You have been my constant friend, my forever companion.
You, truth, are more a part of me than I am of myself.
I feel we've danced this waltz forever, and I try to perfect the steps.
You teach me. I am taught by truth.
Oh, how I love the dance that You lead me in.
I know that You are with me, shielding me from harm.
I am protected by truth.
And You are continually ushering me to happiness, peace, joy,
provision, and every good thing; truth champions me.
How could You be invisible when You are in all, and You are all around?

Tear

A tear cracks the ground,
Unsettles the earth's core,
Disturbs the axis,
Giving acknowledgment to a change that's irrevocable.

A change has manifested,
Shaking the foundation of the earth.
A moment's sacrifice yields
A quake, a new direction, breaking a rule and substituting a plan.

Sacrifice ensures eternal rest.
It affords me an unprecedented grace.
A cascading tear heals every need.
By time introduced the request.

A tear severed old requirements,
Establishing principles fresh and new.
A tear devoured the enemy's canvas
And fulfilled the prophecy of His divine plan.

A tear, ushering benefits and gifts in its wake,
Healed as evidence by a tear that's a tear in the earth
By the One from whom the tear was shed.

The Rainbow

Look at the 'bow.
Our constant reminder that the rain will not mark the end.
A clear representation of the promise and sign of God's return.

The 'bow casts a vivid color array.
Happiness travels the course of its beams.
Over the rainbow is this mystical place.
Folks remember the treasures proposed there.

But listen unto the words I say
As you consider the altered sky.
Best yet to remember the rainbow
As one promise from the One on high.

To wonder if God's words can be tested
As a sign to verify its worth,
Consider the wondrous rainbow,
A sign of a new covenant for the future of earth.

Simple and Elemental Faith

Simple and elemental faith,
Trusting in God always.
Not giving account to situations or surroundings,
Just knowing that God will provide.

Simple and elemental faith
As a child comes forth in unrestrained belief,
Looking unto God as the provider,
Seeking Him as the answer to and for all we seek.

Simple and elemental faith
As a child gazes up at a much-adored Father
Without logic running interference,
Just a predisposition to believe all that He's said.

Simple and elemental faith,
A defendable assertion of Your truth.
I know that my God is always with me,
And He will do all He says He will do.

Childlike faith in believers, possessing an all-enduring childlike faith,
So simple, so elemental, so true.
Greater are these in the kingdom of God
For with a steady and vice-like grip on their faith,
They will fight to maintain the security of that hold.

(Inspired by Matthew 18 KJV.)

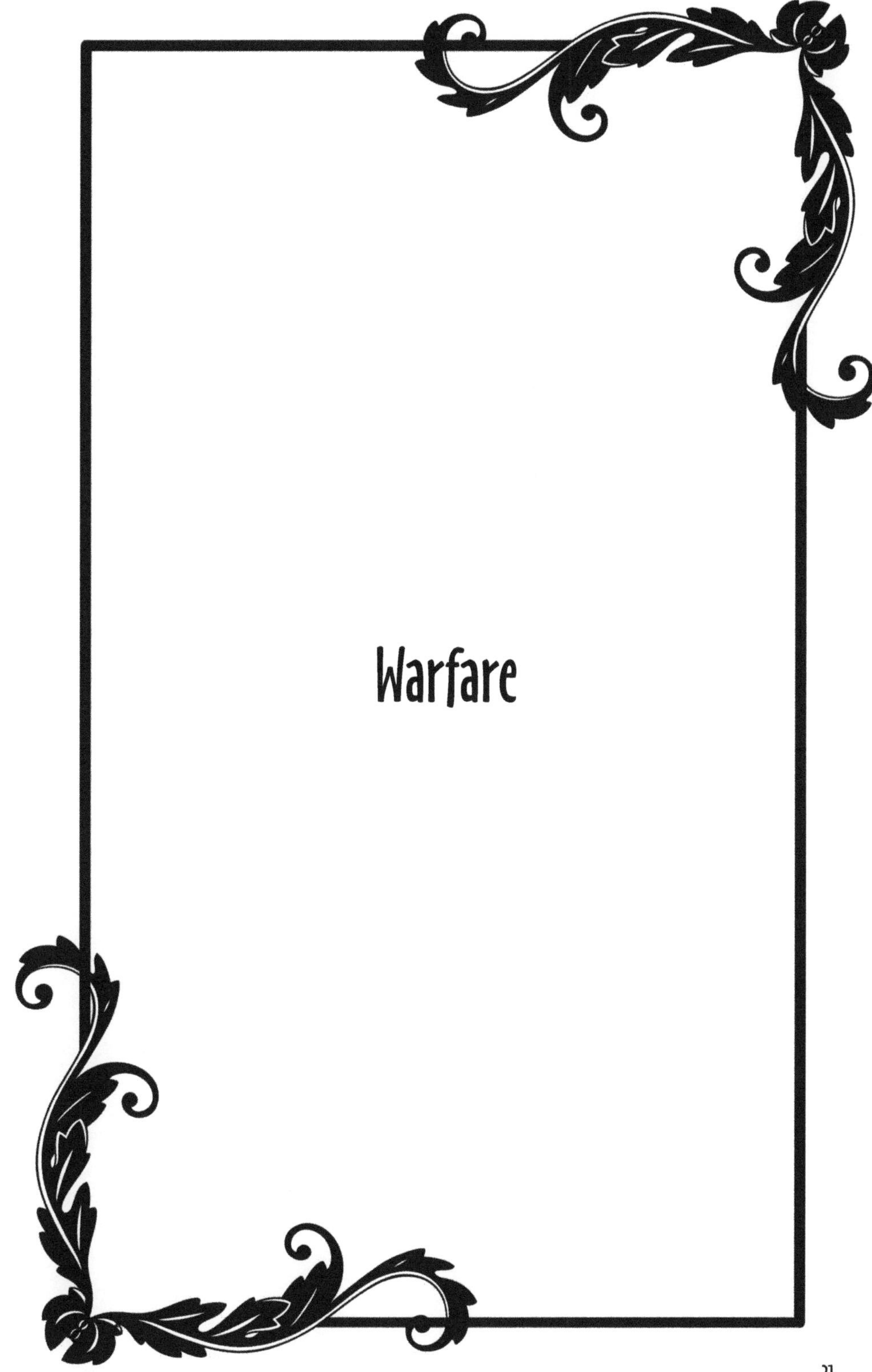

Warfare

A Flesh Fight

A flesh fight.
Why fear and trembling?
Bound with chains, heavy, rusted,
Link upon solid link,
Biting, burning into this flesh,
Hurting, searing, agonizing, relentless pain.
Sores infested, poisoned by chains,
Pestered by pests, crawling, poking, prodding,
At my left hand, at my right.
They have bound my feet;
Weighted balls hinder my steps.
Too heavy to move,
Motionless, draining, muscular atrophy.
Chains attached to break motion.
Chains upon chains, seared, linked by fear and trembling.

One more step.
Weight added.
Try to raise a hand.
Shackle yanked, pulled.
I hear the jangle and snatch my hand back.
A flesh fight.
To lift my head,
To raise my hand,
To walk away from
The fight, the flesh fight,
Links, chains, balls, compounded and compacted,
With great fear and trembling.

Flesh fight, fight flesh.
Fight chains, heavy-laden, burdensome.
Fight the symptoms
That chains caused—
Sores, welts, bleeding, bleeding, bleeding.
Fight cause, fear, worry, flesh derivatives.
Fight accusations, false witness casting, blasting falsehoods
Causing fear in the flesh; my flesh mocking me with fear.

Fight flesh.
Walk the chains off.
Let them be loosened.
Fight to lift the hands,
To work as He called,
To praise through,
To worship through.
Use the chains to strengthen your muscles.
Stretch even harder, raise even higher.
Use the fear as a stepstool.

To walk in a victory over flesh,
Hands raised, legs in motion.
Not on your own.
Can't do it alone,
Can't do it on your own.
A helper is required
To help fight fear,
To help fight worry,
To help fight disobedience,
To help fight.

Helper, helping to fight.
Taking over the limbs
So that I can raise them,
So that I can move,
Move out of fear,
Move out of strongholds.
Helping me to walk by the helper's power,
In His will,
Past my will,
Into my purpose,
Dominating flesh
With power,
With authority,
With my helper in His sovereign power!

Breaking Loose

I wanna break loose.
Break free of this existing, this merely existing,
A merely getting by,
A day-to-day grind,
Going through what is accepted,
Emulating what everyone else has expected,
Trying to convince myself this should be fine for me.

I wanna break loose.
Lose this acceptance of mass replication,
Today shaped as a carbon copy of yesterday.
Not excited about tomorrow because I put the image in place.
Faded newspaper print, revived as the story of today,
Or the adoption of a forged image to be copied and repeated,
Copied and repeated,
Copied and repeated.

I wanna erect a random generation
Of spontaneous blessings, opportunities.
Walking in new levels,
Meeting the capabilities
And the myriad experiences awaiting me.
Make it real for me,
All the dreams and the visions that I see
With a spiritual eye, not naturally.

I wanna fight,
Knock down the walls,
Tear down mediocrity.
Fight for my right stand,
for the solidarity,
the assuredness,
the permanence of His plan.

I wanna fight.
Fight to stay as a permanent receptacle of joy.
Fight to live life, to really live life
With joy overflowing.
To tear off the layers,
The film continually erecting itself,
Distorting the real picture,
To shake things up so that the authentic vision is realized.

The vision is every day.
Not just an image,
Not just a passing fancy, a whimsical desire, a fleeting hope.
Not just a salve for those really hard days,
A placebo to offer fake satisfaction
So mediocrity can continue.

What am I doing wrong?
What am I missing?
What am I not doing,
        not moving in,
                not stepping into?

I wanna break loose,
Axe in hand,
Wielding it purposefully,
Swinging mightily
To cut loose,
To bring down,
Swiftly crashing into the realm of old, of the, "This is okay,"
Embracing the invitation to new.
Each effort to lift the axe a step closer to truth.

A swift kick.
A stamping out and away,
Stamping away the enemy's plans,
Smashing away the lies.

Plans that were built with cunning wiles
From the distracting works of a deceiver.

A blocking deceiver would endeavor to debate a plan
And promote
Reasoning
To cause one to accept defeat,
To accept mediocrity,
To conform to it.
The deceiver offers lies to perpetuate a situation,
A situation that's void of joy and absent from happiness,
A deflector of prosperity.

He whispers a plan away from God's promises.
Softly at first to lay the seed, to establish it.
Watering it with a perception of innocence,
Leading gently with more lies to cause the seed to germinate,
To become commonplace.
He crafts his plan and ushers, nudges, and redirects you to it.
Do you continue to listen?
Do you remain rigidly in the relief and ease of not fighting?
Even though your state of existence is depreciating,
Your allowance of the status quo ever increasing.
Your energy depleted.
The enemy willing you,
Willing you to defeat,
Willing you away from God's will.

I wanna break loose.
Loose from a plan of lies; that's trickery.
My Savior died so that I could live in truth
And overcome the dullness, the disenchantment, the hollowness
Of a mere existence.

I don't believe the lies.
That's why my heart cries out in frustration.
My soul cries out, "Lord, do You hear me?"

I long to effect change
You must have placed this greater expectancy in me.
This different type of expectance that has filled me with urgency.
Otherwise, the common would be my norm.
The common would be my expectation, my balm.
Yet my spirit cries out against the common.

A war wages between soul and spirit,
With a flesh that's willing to walk through the motions.
But a spirit that's highly dissatisfied and constantly waging war
Because it knows that the common is not right, not right for me.

My spirit knows that the common
Does not match what God has instilled in the spirit.
The common does not agree with the promises;
The common cannot understand them, can't grasp the reality of them.
The common does not feel safe when displaced from mediocrity.
It refuses to believe what the heart sees.

The spirit longs to break loose,
To destroy the tether, the bindings that try to hold excellence down.
The spirit longs to break free,
To be everything that God
Constantly calls it to be.
So life is not a struggle in the mundane
But a rejoice and praise in the excellence.

Freed to enjoy a closer walk with God, continually
Freed by His sacrifice.
In constant companionship and guidance,
A praise and worship in the joy of His salvation
And in the life He gifted in love,
An exceptional life here on earth.
A fulfilled life here on earth.
A life loosened for God's plans by faith in His promises.

Cycle End

Cycle, cyclic matters,
Revisiting the same place different times.
Bound in the barriers, self-imparted,
Accepting the trick of the enemy, unchallenged, going around and around.

I cry out to my Lord,
Who provides the help
To burst through the fortress, effortlessly.
To bring back the things taken away from me,
Restoring, blessing, and awaiting the chance to set me free.

Cycle, cyclic matters,
Battle with weapons, not carnal.
Freed by His mighty weapons and knowledge of His promises
As I go around and around in His Word,
Standing firmer and firmer on faith.
Grasping and then holding fast to His promises.
Stamping out doubt and giving all cares to Him,
Soaring in the freedom He gives.
His perfect love ushers me to joy, and my cup overflows.
A new cycle presented—immediately rejected.
My life under new direction—barriers broken, cycle redirected.

Inspired by heartfelt compassion and empathy for my biological sister during her time of loss, but also for my spiritual sisters and brothers in their times of need to suit up and press on in battle.

Suit Up for War

Heart heavy,
Trying to press on past
The confusion, the hurt, the disappointment.
Not knowing which is worse,
The confusion, the hurt, or the disappointment.

Even though my face may not show it right now,
I still love You; I still trust You.
I am just having a hard time letting
      The truth of my love shine brighter
      Than the heaviness that is present within me.

Heart heavy.
Trying to praise,
      And I cry.
Trying to laugh,
      And I cry.
Feeling guilty that I can experience
Any happiness amid such sorrow.

Even though my eyes don't shine quite as brightly right now,
I still love You; I still trust You.
I am just having a hard time letting go of the hurt,
      Seeing beyond a dream
      That was in my grasp
      That is now gone.
      And for this dream not to be.

My heart cries out to You
In the darkness,
"Lord, pull away the clouds.
Help me to put on my armor
Even when I feel that even it is also too heavy.
Help me to praise You,
Giving voice and action
To the fact that
            I still trust You; I still love You."

In earnest I fight now
To place a greater faith in You
Than in my feelings and what
My loss dictates that I feel.

I trust You.
And that trust and reliance and confidence in You
I vow to increase
To bring fruition to the words
That I use
To command my victory
And to overcome the darkness and the spirit of heaviness.

Even if it takes one step at a time,
One humming of one stanza,
One hallelujah,
One song,
One, "Praise You, Jesus,"
I lay this at Your feet.

I take each day as one day,
As another day to be thankful,
Choosing to remember Your goodness
And to thank You for the blessings that I have
            Past, present, and future.

Willing myself to open my eyes with fresh perception
To look upon the faces of the
Hand-picked gifts that You have bestowed upon me
        Time and time again.
I renew my mind and refocus to focus on You.
This is what I choose to do,
Even though my emotions war and rage against me.

My heart,
Praying my way through it,
Declaring the words of my Lord; it's personal.
God, Your promises spew forth,
Declaring my joy for the spirit of this heaviness,
Commanding my strength,
Commanding and declaring everything that
You say
I can have and be.

So even though I am at war,
Even though I fight,
And we are in this war together—You, at the helm—
To reinstate what the enemy has stolen
And shield against what he has tried to steal,
I yet trust You.
I still love You, Lord.
And through this,
I trust
The heaviness to leave,
And I thank You for that
Now, right now,
Even before what I've prayed and declared and wage war against,
Even before the fruition manifests.

Have You Ever?

Have you ever
> Faced a struggle,
> Stared the giant right in his or her face?
> The fear of it seems overwhelming as it tries to take hold.
> You, only able to press on by His grace.

Feels so alone.
> Nobody providing the answers that you need.
> No one understanding just what you face.
> You try to explain it, but no one really gets it.

Yet you are searching,
> Trying to find a word to offer relief from your pain,
> Seeking a word to let you know that you *will* overcome,
> That everything will be all right,
> Even as it appears that no one can provide your answers.
> It appears that no one can lead you out of
> the war that you are fighting.

It's at this time that you realize there is only one who can help,
> Only one who has the answers you seek,
> Only one who has the light to set your steps to flight
>> In the right direction,
>> Out of the darkness,
>> Into His marvelous light.

At times like these, only God remains.
Seek His counsel first.
He will assist so that your search is not in vain.

You have to seek Him for yourself in times like these.
> Seek His Word.
> Seek Him for wisdom.
> Seek His understanding.
> Seek His promises.
> Seek His answers; He will reveal what to do!

I Come Out

I come out of a place where need was great,
Encumbered with great troubles, trials, bordering on despair.
In a moment where no one knew or could provide an answer
Or a shred of relief,
You reminded me of peace.
The peace You left for me.
The peace You gave to me.
You granted me peace.

I come out of a sense of waning hope.
Out of a longing to lift my hands up in surrender
Unto the events as they unfold around me.
Unable to withstand the weight of the burdens
I alone attempted to bear,
You held me up.

I come out of a moment when
I realized that no one knew enough
Or could see enough into my pain.
Of those who trivialized my trials
Without knowing from whence
The cause of my pain lay.

"It's relative," they say.
No, it is not.
Not when in the midst of my pain
I hear silence.

The air motionless.
The environment void of anything discernable,
And all emphasized, all highlighted by
Silence.

Time seems suspended, concentrated on a moment.
Moment extended, dragging, stretching,
Looping back around until you can't really tell if time has gone by.
Are you at the start of the trial?
Are you in the middle of the test, near the end?
Time in this barren land seems immeasurable.
It just lingers on.

I longed for answers, begged and pleaded for them,
Carried away above my circumstances.
So if the answer came in the whirlwind of my emotions,
I didn't hear it.
In the thickness of the dark, threatening clouds, I couldn't see it.
In the climax of the fight
You gave me comfort beyond understanding
That I may rest, rest only in You.

I come out of a place where
Only God remained
    To see me through my pain,
    To see me through my frailties,
    To provide strength for me, and
    Lead me to joy and holy rest.
God, You carried me.

So with renewed hope, with faith, with trust and belief,
I am lifted.
I float above what's going on around me.
You have reenergized me, filled me up, empowered me.

You surrounded me in a love above anything I could ever deserve.
A love so strong that light,
Light overwhelms,
Agitates,
And attacks the silence.

Thunderous sounds embrace my heart
And my mind
With Your love.
Taking the muzzle from my mouth, releasing the clamps
So I can worship and praise You with my voice.

The mobility, the energy is reawakened in me.
I am charged by Your power.
Hands and heart no longer weighed down but lifted
And reaching higher.
When only yesterday could only see lower,
You empower me
And
I come out!

Monumental

Monumental: That's the scope of adversity formed.
A churning of darts designed with unpleasant
Plans, destructive intentions.
Pressure builds, gaining strength, surging and
Releasing the force that propels,
Aggravating the intensity of the situation: Confusion arises.

Bombarding my mind with futile thoughts
Of dead works and impossibilities,
Chanting and challenging that I can't, I won't, I'll never.

Monumental: That's the size of the storm I face.
Gale-force winds attack, and the onslaught of the
Ensuing storm attempts to obscure my vision
So that I can't see clearly.
Ravaging my purpose, pilfering from my destined prosperity
As I merely gaze ahead, stumped by idleness.

The fierce, blinding storm forges on, commanding a deafening noise
That attempts to cut off and block my hearing,
Rendering me unable to hear Your voice.

Monumental: That's the power You've authorized unto me.
Your Word holds the blueprint detailing my victory.
I reign and rule because You've laid out the course of my destiny.
I'm no longer bound unless I allow myself to be.

You impart the ability to overcome life's storms,
To claim the victor's walk.
I walk on,
Knowing and confessing
That before the fight begins, with You, I've already won!

So the weapons that form and storm and rage,
Though great in size and momentum,
They are weakened in the wake of my worship and praise to You.
And in the wake of my testimony to Your power,
Those storms, though once powerful in size and strength,
Are now unable to gain ground, hold me bound, or prosper.
No, they won't prosper!

Shake Off

To shake off the blanket,
The second layer of skin,
Ever-present, taunting, tantalizing, tempting,
Lying dormant only to rise up again,
New positioning, new angles,
Shake off the dust from the blanket.
Fresh fire for the long road.

Superhuman

Superhuman
By the supernatural Spirit within me,
Empowered to transcend the norm
And to escape and overcome life's limitations.
Superhuman
Because that's God's gift to me.

Acceptance of the gift of His Son,
Jesus, the best gift to me.
Receiving the gift of His power,
Holy Spirit's power infused into me.

I possess power to trample the enemy.
I stamp out defeat because victory is etched into me.
I speak life to resurrect dead areas.
I call upon the power, and it surges forth
To free victims from captivity.

I'm superhuman.

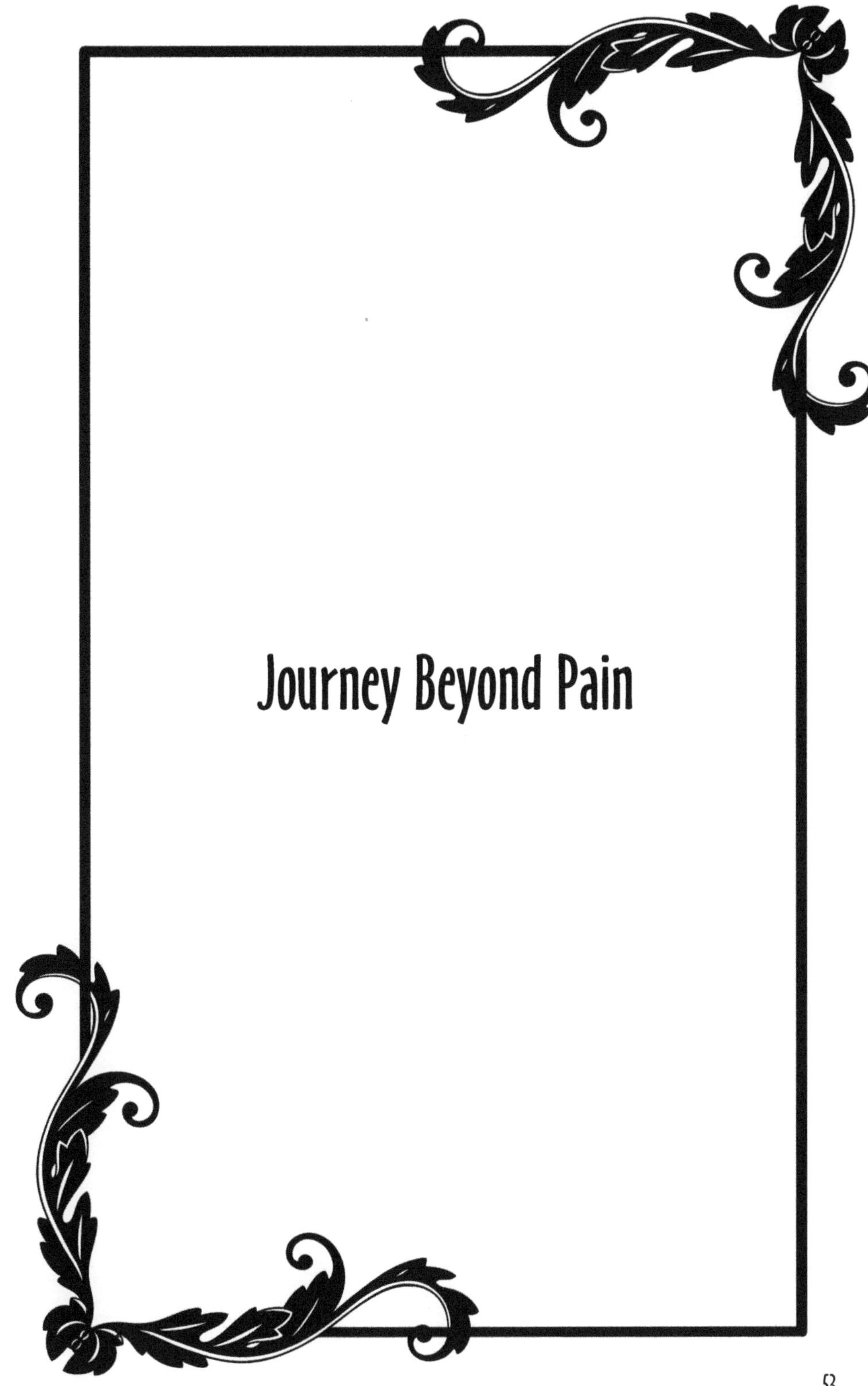

Journey Beyond Pain

A Glimpse through Pain

When you are tired of pain
And are "going through."
When you want to cry,
But it hurts physically to do so.

When you are afraid to sleep,
Even though you've prayed,
Even though you've been prayed over,
Even though you believe for your healing.

But when you close your eyes to finally sleep,
You are startled awake,
Gasping for air,
Body jerking,
Heart hammering in your chest,
Trying to hold on to this belief,
The faith in the words, "I'm healed."

Confessing and believing that
I should sleep in peace
But startled awake,
Gasping for breath,
Pain in side,
Body jerking,
Heart hammering in chest.

Awake now!
Read the Word,
Pray the Word,
Praise on my own
In the dark hours of the night.
Worship until my momentum runs dry; I'm tired.
Watch the Word in action.

Drift off to sleep.
Startled awake,
Gasping for air,
Pain in side, soreness intensified,
Body jerking,
Heart hammering in chest.
What now?

What do I do in the midst,
In the precarious place, that suspension of time
Between declaration and manifestation of healing?

No spirit of fear.
Lay down in peace; how?
When my body betrays my confession,
And as much as I want to cry,
It hurts too much physically to do so.

New complication.
Now medical intervention.
Fear knocking,
Breath betraying.
Then I see them—
My pain forgotten.

I am not one who has no hope.
Prayers for people in the hospital
Who seem far worse than me.
Bodies bruised and broken,
Eyes vacant yet longing,
Longing as they appear to have no hope.

"God heal you and bless you," I leave in parting.
Silent prayer for you, Mister.
Silent prayer for you, Miss.
Healing for you, young lady,
And I mean it!

Looking into eyes that show loneliness,
Vacant, black, yearning eyes—
Lost, wondering, beckoning eyes—shadows.
Shadows in the depth, shadows in the periphery.
Confined without strength or knowledge or hope to remove restraints.

Heal them, Lord, Lord, that they may know You,
Your bruises for them,
Your stripes for them,
Your love to them, God, manifested; shower
And rain Your light down on them!

I pray for them
In the midst of pain.
Pain that I have faith to be freed from.
I have hope to be freed from pain.
I must have faith!

How would I believe it for them, desire healing for them,
Request and declare it for them
If I didn't believe it for myself,
Even amid pain,
As I wait for manifestation of healing?

In tears I think of my uncle,
To have known pain more intense than this.
In tears, I think of my cousin, so young, of days
Where breath fought to evade her.
In tears, I think of them all
When pain steals slumber,
When unassisted by temporary easement,
And when pain fights faith.
With differing views on the battlefield,
Chants of, "I will be healed,"
To I am at peace, I am healed,
Even amid the prayers and the pain!

Stunned

Stunned
Because what I expected to happen
Did not come to pass.
In the praying and actions put forth,
The result painted a totally different picture.

Baffled,
Trying to figure out
What went wrong,
What could have been done differently.
How could this be the outcome
When the components of the formula were carefully followed?

Drained.
Worked really hard.
Dotted all the proverbial Is, crossed all the Ts.
Pushed through, though weary.
Now, left depleted.
       Energy zapped.
       Focus blurred.

Stumped,
Wondering, *What are the next steps?*
Which way do I go?
Whom do I turn to?
Should I change directions?
Should I stay peering at the growing height of the barrier
Stretched out before me?
Its length and heights I am unable to see.
It grows and stretches beyond my periphery.

Yet I am resolved
To throw my hands up,
To get myself out of the way,
To fully and finally give to You

What I said I would.
        What I thought I did,
                But evidently I still held on to.
And to look past the image of what this current picture shows.

I am committed,
Still committed to trust in You,
Knowing that although I struggled with disappointment,
You will see me through this.
And even though a lack of energy, a lack of zeal, a lack of gusto
Have surrounded me and robbed me and placed
Lead weights on my ability to press forward,
This, too, shall work for my good.

As I release my hands and invite You to do Your work,
You, I welcome to pick me up and take me where I need to go,
        Where I need to be.
You, supplying me with energy with strength with power,
Recharging my batteries and giving me a new path, a better
Path, a bypass to get to where You want me to go.

I will continue to praise and worship my way
Through the murkiness of my situation
And on over into the clarity and the light—to You.

Jaded without You
(In memory of Uncle "Pop" Willie Irving Brinson.)

The world seems jaded.
It's lost its hue.
It's a little shaded; my life's lost some color without you.

Earth feels tilted, perhaps lifted off its axis.
Simple things changed.
Sugar doesn't taste as sweet.
The melody of birds singing escapes me.
The sweetness of fragrance evades me.
Life is a road of blandness, void of lasting flavor.
My focus is blurred.

The world seems a little jaded.
It just doesn't seem right.
Feels like I am living someone else's life,
Going through the motions, the motions, the motions.
An instant replay, a reenactment of yesterday.

My experience is just a little cloudy.
I'm waiting for the sun to break through.
What I felt I knew of life
Has lost an important ingredient—
The element of you.

I want the color back in my life—
Not another zombie-like, fictitious day—
To see sparks fly around my life,
To have the wind bear me up and not toss me around.

Usher in Your Spirit, Lord.
Only You will do.
The joy of the Lord is my strength.
I meditate on those words to recreate that joy in me.
The colors of life, in me renew.

Awaken the vibrant colors of life.
Repaint the pictures for me.
Bring forth the light in vision.
This canvas is too dismally lit to be.

Shake up this world of me.
Put the planets back in alignment.
Make this again the world I viewed in beauty.
Let me see the beauty that fled away.

The brilliance of color I always loved.
Let me experience it above this heaviness.
Lord, splash on me
All the colors that I miss.
Heal this need in me.
Free me in Your closeness, Your proximity.
Soak me, baptize me in the colors of Your love.

> To appoint unto them that mourn in Zion, to give unto them beauty for ashes, the oil of joy for mourning, the garment of praise for the spirit of heaviness; that they might be called trees of righteousness, the planting of the LORD, that he might be glorified. (Isa 61:3 KJV)

> Then he said unto them, Go your way, eat the fat, and drink the sweet, and send portions unto them for whom nothing is prepared: for this day is holy unto our Lord: neither be ye sorry; for the joy of the Lord is your strength. (Neh. 8:10 KJV)

> The Lord is my strength and my shield; my heart trusted in him, and I am helped: therefore my heart greatly rejoiceth; and with my song will I praise him. (Ps. 28:7 KJV)

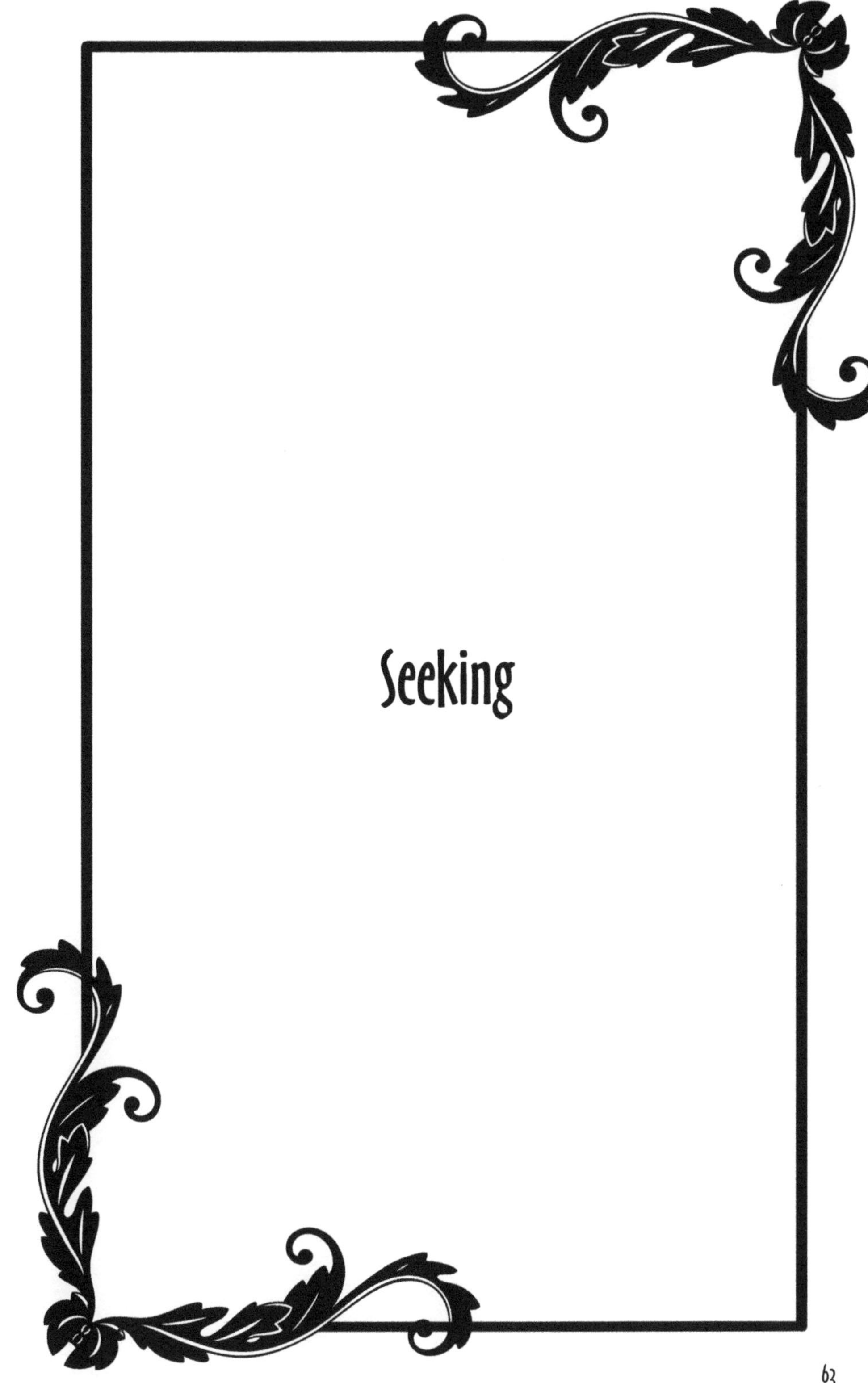

Seeking

My Life Is in Your Word

I try to find the outline to the steps that I take.
I try to see beyond the horizon spread before me.
I try to realize my dreams beyond what I see and know.
I try to hold firmly to my beliefs.

Your Word says abundant life is for me.
I stand, awaiting orders for action, patiently,
Obedient to Your command,
Expecting Your instruction for my life.
My life to live, Your joy, in me, fulfilled,
To start anew and really experience the life You drew out for me!

My life is in your Word,
Spelled out in your plan.
My life is in Your Word.

When I need a way made out of no way,
My life is in Your Word.
When I need a word, a revelation in a midnight hour,
My life is in Your Word.
When I need what seems out of my reach,
My life is in Your Word.

To feel the joy, to live Your truth,
To receive Your wisdom and instruction,
My life is in Your Word.
The Word of God yields life!

My Steps

My steps I see before me.
I see them clearly outlined in grace.
The peace that once escaped me,
I grab it firmly.
It's mine,
And I take it!

Speak to Me

Gaze upon the magnificence.
The beauty of His holiness is far too great to behold.
Reflect upon His goodness.
Testimonies too countless to be told.

Marvel at His loving-kindness.
He rains forth new mercies daily.
Bow down to holy splendor.

Speak to me, Lord Jesus.
I need to hear from You.
An echo in the distance vibrates;
I thought it was a word from You.

Speak to me, Lord Jesus.
I want to hear all You have to say.
Your words I esteem very highly.
It is manna for my day.

Speak to me, Lord Jesus.
Without Your voice, my lifeline is gone.
I pull on You for goings and comings,
To direct me as to which I belong.

Speak to me, Lord Jesus.
I beg this as an earnest cry.
Your voice caressing my mind, my heart
As a beautifully longed for and much-treasured lullaby.

Transition

My life is in transition.
I teeter over the precipice.
Do I go blindly over the edge,
Not seeing what lies ahead?

I admit that right now, I hate this feeling!
I long for release,
To escape the unknown; it scares me.
I long to know all and to embrace a perfect peace.

The fear of the Lord is the beginning of knowledge.
Wisdom is He, the Holy Word is He, and He is wisdom.
So am I seeking a crystal ball's picture for me
Instead of placing total trust in You?

We say we trust You and
Wait patiently for Your call.
But as my life stands in transition,
When You call, will I step out
And trust You to guide my walk?

He will keep you in perfect peace
If your mind and heart are stayed on Him.
That answer seems simple, uncomplicated,
Stress-free, and weightless.

If it's so simple, why is it hard to enact?
Why the struggle and questioning why?
Hmm? An answer right there before me,
My faith in the Word to put it to work.

My life is in transition.
I must confess that I teeter on the edge,
To push past a fear and deny it,
To allow Your Spirit to comfort and guide me.

Shake away the devil's grasp on my peace
And allow Your Spirit to comfort and safely guide me!

Transition, some people say, is a good thing.
I pray these people are wiser than me
Because as I stand at the edge of this precipice,
What's over the edge, I cannot clearly see.
I can only trust in You and Your Word while
I face this, my life in transition.

> The fear of the Lord is the beginning of knowledge: but fools despise wisdom and instruction. (Prov. 1:7 KJV)

Unsettled

Unsettled by the events unfolding,
Serenity is absent from its scope.
Pieces fly around haphazardly.
Direction shifts in the cosmos.
Plans abandoned or not thought of,
Wandering from pillar to post.

In search of guidance,
Am I making the right move?
Is this Your will for me?
Is this the right relationship?
Is this the right job?
Should I go forward with this decision, or should I pursue that one?
Am I taking on too much?

Praying again and again,
Yet the same questions are posed.
All along you remain unsettled.
You step out in the direction that you think you should go.
Or is it the direction you wish you could go.
And you feel as if you don't know which way is right.
With hands raised in frustration, you ponder your plight.

Unsettled by the events unfolding.
Serenity is absent from its scope.
Pieces fly around haphazardly.
Direction shifts in the cosmos.
Plans abandoned or not thought of,
Wandering from pillar to post.

Could it be that the answer you seek
Is evidenced by you being unsettled?
Do you believe in what you're asking for?
Do you have faith that your answers are being heard?
The step you took causes more unease,

So you must ask yourself, as you follow a lead,
Who heads up the lead directing those steps
That have left in its wake an unsettled state?

Is it you who you are following, heeding your own advice
Even when you've asked the Lord,
And what you're doing just doesn't seem right.
Are you disregarding His direction, His prompting, His lead?
It could pinpoint the reason to you being unsettled.

To counter the plight, deactivate that state.
Reverse the direction, so there is peace in the midst of the storm.
Let Holy Spirit guide you.
He orders the steps of the righteous,
So the pieces fit together, and God's plan is revealed.
And when your steps, ordered by faith in Holy Spirit.
Can be walked with joy unspeakable and full of glory,
Even when you don't know exactly where each step leads,
You know that each step works for your good in the end.

And you can move on with that joy, riding shotgun,
Settled in the faith of God's love,
Settled in the knowledge of His truth
That Jesus died and rose again for our sins.
Settled in the knowledge that He did not leave us as orphans,
Settled in His leaving our Guide.
If you need His guidance, you can just ask
For the power to keep you settled and on the right path.

Peel into My Vision

Peel into my vision.
Discover the layers inside.
God has defined my purpose,
Revealed through the levels where my faith resides.

The plan that He has for me
Coincides with my capacity to believe
As He carries away each scale to reveal
The next steps I need to pursue.

Peel into my vision
And know a little more about me.
A desire to know what makes me happy
Is to see the fruition of God's plan for me.

> For I know the thoughts that I think toward you, saith the Lord,
> thoughts of peace, and not of evil, to give you an expected end.
> (Jeremiah 29:11 KJV)

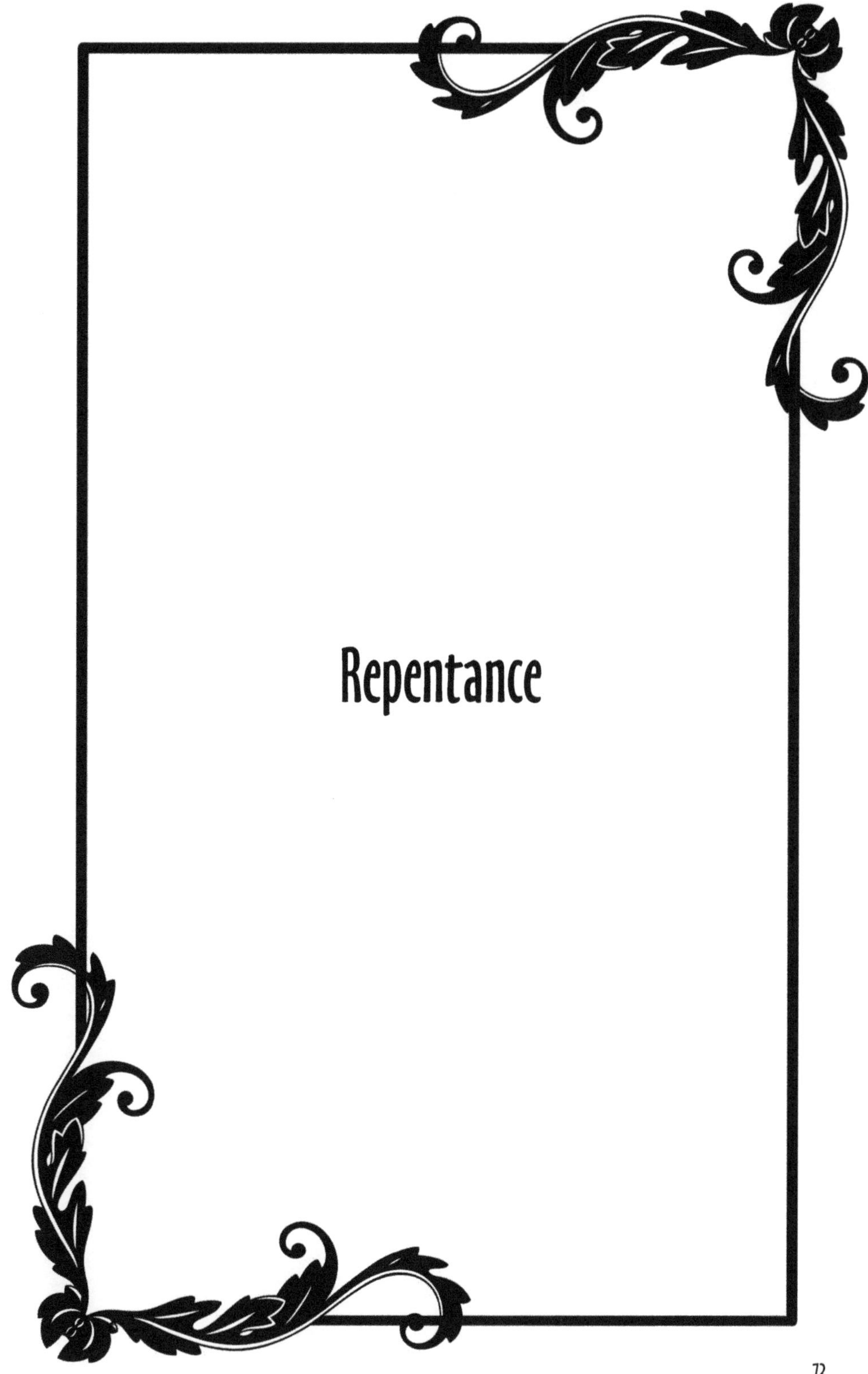

Repentance

A Turn

Why get mad and turn away
As if He did something wrong?
Why not handle disappointment, disagreements in a better way?
Isn't there a better way?

Is it an excuse to do what you want to do anyway?
Are you waiting for an opportunity,
For a supposed "mess up,"
To give you a reason to turn away?

To ignore your present situation
And escape into a world that brings self-glory and justification,
Making things right in your own eyes?
But what about your heart?
In your heart you know if there are buried lies.

It is because you are blinded and transfixed by
The falsehood that you've created for yourself,
A fictional realm,
An unreality that,
After being played out,
You come back.

You come back to yourself
And see that you are right back at the very beginning.
You've gone nowhere;
You've accomplished nothing.

Except the fact that you turned your back
And are now sorry,
And you want to restore the relationship.
But instead of admitting the fault in yourself,
You fault Him, never even admitting your fault against Him.

So how can you expect to restore the relationship
If you keep blaming someone else,
When it is you who turned your back?

Turn
your back
again.
"What?" you ask.

First, get yourself right, in right standing.
Admit and confess your faults.
Acknowledge just whom you sinned against,
Then you can be in a state to ask for forgiveness
And restore the relationship.

Forgiveness comes easily for Him.
His grace covers it. His love covers it.
He loves you.
He will forgive you, forgiveness birthed out of
His giving heart and His grace.
A clean slate given.

But when times get rough—and they just may—
Don't be so quick to turn away from Him
And wind up in that same old, dry, dead, barren place.
Be mindful of self.
Heed instruction from Him, the One who can guide you.
Toward Him is the one direction in which you should always turn.

I Shirk Off

I shirk off every garment,
Cloaked in shame,
In the mires of darkness,
Of unbidden vices that besot me.

Layer upon layer fashioned
On me, weighing me down,
Covering my form.
It made my form unrecognizable.

I peel off those layers that I didn't want.
But they were offered to me, and I did take them.
Those layers, I shirk off
As I break free from the bondage that each layer represents.

As each experience sought to brand me
With a false ownership,
Coming and demanding an authority,
When to it, authority does not belong.

I shed those layers,
Allowing the me that is hidden beneath them
To spring forth.

I rise forth above the layers,
Hovering as I ascend to the appointed place,
Where God's glory in me shines forth
As the me that He created me to be is revealed, making its holy debut.

Images

Images.
Images dance around.
They fly around haphazardly
From different angles,
In different frames,
At varying speeds.
Crowding the mind with—these images.
Pressing the very same images
To produce thoughts and
Then thought patterns
To crowd out clear thoughts
To be replaced with images that a thief purports.

Images.
They rewrite the tracks of your mind,
Rewiring your circuitry,
Replacing the old contents of what you've known-or thought you knew.
The contents placed there previously to free your mind.
Those contents that you don't use anymore, easily neglected.
The contents placed there to help you
To fight the infiltration,
The disease,
The addictions
Stamped there
By an image-maker,
An illustrator,
An illusionist
Trying to redesign your thought life,
Trying to reconstruct your faith life—rewired.
Redesigned with impressions
By creating these
Images.

These images, influenced by sounds,
Amplified and magnified by sound.
Overcoming and overwriting the purposed placeholder—
The faith placeholder—
And to be filled with weapons, not carnal
Instruments to keep you clear and strengthened
Slots that should be for
Right thoughts,
Good thoughts,
Good memories,
Good reasoning
To replace negative reasoning and fleshly thoughts.
Images placed there, transplanted images,
Images with a desire to clear out, smear, and reprogram a clean mind.

Images.
Images have sound.
Do you not hear the sounds
That those images inject,
That those images speak
As they whisper
And cajole
And tempt
Amid their silence?

The images that say it's okay
Just this one time.
No one has to know.
Or the image that says
You are not good enough.
You'll never be good enough.
You'll never make it.
It's too big.
It's too hard.
Nobody loves you!
Nobody cares.

Images crowd the mind,
But who takes ownership?
Who put them there?
What are their purposes,
These particular images that transform thought
And give birth to sin?

Whether sin of worry beyond doubt
Or lust or fear,
Or of idolatry, pride, lying.
Whatever.
Who stamped those images there
To fill up the voided or empty swept clean memory banks,
Or the dusty, unused, and overwritten, now jumbled Word that was
Planted there once; but no longer used, faith dimmed?
Or the info there is not recognizable; you can't identify it.
Or the images make it difficult to identify with it.

It's coming too fast, too often.
It's too crowded now, crowded with junk, garbage; you can't decipher it.
You don't know where it came from, so you don't trust it.
You don't know what's good or bad.
You can't understand what to keep and what to throw away.
It's been there too long; it's made itself a home.
And although jumbled, confusing, frustrating, and unclear,
You struggle to break free from it; you've had it so long.
Or was that Word from way back when, just holding temporary residence.
Or that Word that once had taken root, appears
To have been deleted bit by bit.
So what's left is available space,
An available home.

So it's free to be overwritten or rewritten by
Images that erupt, bursting forth.
You chose accept
When the request was first presented.
This harmless image that

The whisperers tell you that you can control.
But that part that once spoke to you has
Already been overwritten in your mind
Because your flesh speaks louder
And has filled that slot already
With the image of—
Self-importance,
Pride,
Self-indulgence.

In the midst, a struggle.
An old, barely visible, image flickers.
The simmering vestiges of the image ignites,
It awakens.
It calls,
Telling you that this collage of misshapen images is wrong.
But you quickly cast it aside
Because that is just not the image that you want,
Not the image you desire right now.
So you place a different picture
In the frame
At the exact same spot
Where resisting the temptation was to reside.

Clear the images, erase them,
Clear my mind.
"Let me be free," you cry.
"Holy Spirit, help me.
How do I do it without You.
I need Your strength, Your help
To replace these images encased in sound that crowd my mind."

These images lie.
They simply and intricately lie.
They hurt.
They leave you weakened.
Abandoned.

Alone.
Traveling a road in darkness, without directions,
Without signs, without company.

Only the sharp angles of the images encased in frames.
Dead bolted.
Oh, wait.
That's just another image
masking lies.
Because I am really not alone.
You are really not alone.
God said He would never leave you or forsake you.
God said He would never leave you or forsake you.
God said He would never leave you or forsake you.

Don't you know images have power to transform
What you should really see?
The power to cast an image of what you want to
See or what the enemy wants you to see.
What power will you let reign?
The enemy hates you; this please do see.

Images make it seem desirable
And transform to show in full range of motion pictures of
The script from the deceptive illustrator, the master manipulator,
To get you to believe or buy into.
Selling you a script with a tainted cast; those
Under his employ have adopted his vision.
They aim to promote division of you and truth.
And the plot and the climax of this play that the cast out cast acts out
Is to enslave and then kill you.
Death, eternal separation, is the enemy's goal.
Images are the tools used.

Yet you ask,
"Is it as easy as it's written
To destroy the lying image,

To replace it with whatever is
True,
Honest,
Just,
Pure,
Lovely,
Of good report?"
I am to think on these things.

Sometimes this is difficult.
What if all I've seen,
Or all I see,
Is wrong, is dark?
What if life has been so hard for me,
And the images support this cloudy view
So that darkness and struggle are all I feel I can see?

Or what if I've tried it?
Images removed and came back.
Pretty pictures painted but not lasting.
Old image remains.
Then you question,
"Did the image ever leave,
Or was it in sleep mode,
Like the scriptures you heard in church
Or wrote down but never revisited?"
Did you really want the images to go?
They've been with you so long, these images.
Or did you convince yourself,
Were you telling yourself that they were gone
So that you could keep them at bay,
Save a little for later, save this familiar,
Come back to it when trying and walking that faith walk gets too hard?

A clear mind,
Away from the fake images.
A clean mind,

Cleansed and filled with the Word of God.
Filled with the truth to purge,
To purify,
To provide a clean sweep,
To clear away anything not like His mind,
To leave in its wake holy images.
Empowerment,
Peace,
Removing the gnawing tumor of the enemy's images.

Images may give birth to sound,
Presenting a silent film.
They may shout out that it's impossible.
They may replay the times when you failed.
And again, the question remains,
"Who would supply that image?
Who would replay an image that tempts and then condemns
When there is no condemnation for those who are in Christ Jesus?
When the voice of the enemy you should not hear or obey?"
And likewise, you should not give credence,
give an eye to, or give an ear to these
Images.

Images that are against the Word of God.
Cast down imaginations and
Every high thing that exalts itself against the knowledge of God
To clear the mind,
To clean and purge.
Know the Word to discern the images.
Pray the Word; declare what He said.
Hear the Word to transform the sounds.
Praise God, He inhabits the praises of His people.
Worship God!
Worship God!

Worship God who is always with you. He is on your side.
Worship and give thanks that the Creator of all things has power,
dominion, authority, and control over everything, even images.
And when the road seems long, the fight seems hard—oh, so
hard—and the image is not where His Word and promises say
they should be, press replay, and keep doing it all over again.

Know the Word to discern the images.
Pray the Word; declare what He said.
Hear the Word to transform the sounds.
Praise God, He inhabits the praises of His people.
Worship God!
Worship God!

> Finally, brethren, whatsoever things are true, whatsoever things
> are honest, whatsoever things are just, whatsoever things are pure,
> whatsoever things are lovely, whatsoever things are of good report;
> if there be any virtue, and if there be any praise, think on these
> things. (Phil. 4:8 KJV)

> There is therefore now no condemnation to them which are in
> Christ Jesus, who walk not after the flesh, but after the Spirit.
> (Rom. 8:1 KJV)

> Casting down imaginations, and every high thing that exalteth
> itself against the knowledge of God, and bringing into captivity
> every thought to the obedience of Christ; (2 Cor. 10:5 KJV)

> But thou art holy, O thou that inhabitest the praises of Israel.
> (Ps. 22:3 KJV)

Lost Way

Have you ever lost your way
While traveling the road that's right, or that seems right?
Perhaps you made a wrong turn or veered too far left.
You then look around and realize that you are not where you belong.
Or that you are not where you thought you should be.

Have you ever suddenly felt out of place
When in a place you always go?
Have you felt disconnected and out of order
Standing in a room unknown and spinning with
The sensation of confusion, of being lost?

Is it scary? Frightening? In this abyss of your situation,
Because you took a step too far away from home,
Or forgot where home was,
Or forgot to whom you belong?

Just make another turn, a 180 back home
Into the open arms where our Father resides.

He will show you the way back.
His grace is sufficient.
He will make light your steps.
Each step you make coming ablaze with His light.
As you step in His way, He will add light to your path
And guide you to the haven of peace and joy, His peace and joy.

And in His welcoming joy to see you back home,
He doesn't count against you the fact that you went away.
He won't blame you or make you feel bad or unworthy.
He will embrace you and celebrate your choice to turn to the right way,
So you will not feel bound and condemned for
Having gotten lost in the first place.

And he said unto me, My grace is sufficient for thee: for my strength is made perfect in weakness. Most gladly therefore will I rather glory in my infirmities, that the power of Christ may rest upon me. (2 Cor 12:9 KJV)

One Last Time

I'm gonna try this one last time before I "get right"
Just to get it out of my system.
I know that when I do it today,
I can then keep the urges at bay.

I know what I am supposed to do.
I don't really need to hear it from you.
Given the chance, I can use the Word.
Just as well as, if not better, than you.

I just need a chance to eradicate
These urges to eliminate,
To shake it, and prove that I'm ready.
And then you will see that what I say is true.

I'm gonna try this thing I'm in just one more time before I walk right.
Appease this appetite
For things that I know in my heart that I don't need.

Just one more time.
Just one more try.
Just one more dance.
This *is* my last time.

I can do it.
I can shake it off
After I seal the deal and get some closure.
I am strong enough; I know this.
I can release it just when I choose to.

Don't preach to me like you know,
Like you know more about me and where my heart lies.
I know all about the things I'm in, much, much better than you.
There are no blinders covering my eyes.

I need to do this on my own,
Not for you, but for me!
And all your judgmental, superficial, superior-believing,
self-justified hypercriticalness is only reflecting hate on me.

Makes me want to get and stay away from you
And all the things that you do.
The things that you do for show.
But to me, love you never show.

You secretly rejoice in the things I'm in.
Your heart hates to see me win.
Quick to announce to anyone, my wrongs,
Never acknowledging when I'm right and doing right.
Slickly sliding in a version of your truth and
hiding your hand just as quickly.

You make me want to do this one last time,
Right before I give it up.
It's been with me for such a long time.
I feel like it's family now,
True family, a true friend, like it's the only
real that I can believe and stand in.

Giving it up feels lonely somehow.
I can count on it much more than you
To fill this need, this oh-so-powerful need
That I've been laboring through.

I'm going to get it together.
I know I've got work to do.
But I can't do it right now.
Gotta get ready somehow.

I am still trying to figure this one out,
To try this one more day before I get right.

I know that this is my last day.
I am ready for the change.

I know there are big plans in store for me.
I know blessings are waiting on me.
I know I am gifted.
I've seen that I've got power.

I've seen a future for me that goes beyond
What I've ever hoped for,
Beyond my capacity to believe.
And that vision, it scares me; I'll admit that.

Seems too big for me,
Too big to achieve.
Quite honestly, I didn't even want all that,
All that you've shown me.

Spotlight shines on me.
The heat of the glare, "I'm not ready," I readily declare.
A lot of spotlight on me,
Scrutinizing me, magnifying my every imperfection.
And the way that you do it now, all self-righteously!

Thinking you are better than me.
Likened to a bug squirming under your microscope.
The lens—oh, the glare—the heat of your lens.
Analyzing, tearing apart, dissecting every piece of me.
Not to understand, not to help but to feed your own insecurities.

So that's why I have to get it outta my system.
Just this one last time before I get right.
Then you'll see the me
That I want to shine.
The me that I long to be,
To be that on my own; it seems too hard for me just now.

But when I'm ready, you *will* see the me
That, when magnified through the lens of self-righteousness
Hypocrisy, and hate,
All will see the reflected image of the One who
Originally designed me to be great.

The One who says that I am capable
Because He put ability in me.
The One who says that I am worthy
Because He defines my worth, and
The One who loves me and assures me that with Him, I can do all things.

But I feel like I've gotta get right first.
It's what I feeeeel!

When I get right
Just this one more time.
This one more season.
When the stars line up.
When the taste has gone out of my mouth.
When I no longer desire their approval.
When I no longer want to prove something.
When I find what I've been searching for.
When I get rid of this need.
When I can get there on my own.
When I can leave this stuff alone.

And I can!
I know the power is in me.
I can feel it; its intensity pleads with me.
I am a friend of God's.
He has my back.
I love the Lord,
And He loves me.
I hear Him calling my name.
My Father speaks to me.

And when I finish all this busyness,
I will increase the volume of my hearing and not turn a deaf ear anymore,

You see, His love convicts me.
I don't feel right trying the things that I do to feel right.
I just need this last time.
This last pick-me-up.
This last feel good.
This last validation to get it out of my system.
Then I'll get right.

I will.
You'll see.
And I'll be amazing.
And I'll amaze you.
And you'll see the power of God in me.
Just wait.
Right after I have this one last time.
This one time of relying on me instead of Him.
(I hope I can get there.)

Plague

There is a plague that torments humankind.
Like locusts to destroy all the harvest,
It creeps in and slowly takes control,
Shattering all your gain into mere ash and worthlessness.

There is a plague that just hangs around,
Bringing disease and pestilence in its wake.
It is wired to take all that's good in a thing
And rot away at it until it's not even worth looking upon.

When it is covered in decay and a sight not worthy to behold,
With a stench that causes the stomach to revolt,
Behold the light that stands in its place,
Making the unseemly, viewable again.

Plagues persist through the ages, an iniquity that persists
To generations anew from what was past.
But a precious Lamb was slain,
Covering our doorposts with a varnish that's bloodstained,
Healing and delivering, so we can have a relationship again.

Truth in the Inner Being

Clean, like freshly laundered clothing,
Pure as the emergent, fire-engulfed silver.
Give it so that I may have truth,
Your truth in my inner being.

Truth, pure and undefiled,
Unblemished, not tarnished, not cloaked in deceit or worn.
Not bruised and broken, as on the wings of this emotion.
The result of what defection brings.

Clean, like the aura of a new morning's dew,
Pure and serene as the soft descent of freshly driven snow.
Release it so that I may know truth,
Your truth in my inner being

In the wisdom gleaned from the understanding of Your Word,
Yielding the fruit of truth,
Can I bind truth to gird my loins?
Can I have Your truth to preserve me and help me resist.

Clean, like the cool refreshing breeze of Your anointing,
Like the bliss in the joy of my salvation.
Help me to know Your truth, to live it.
To possess Your truth always in my inner being.

Overflow my cup.
Your truth in my inner being
That I may stay clean guided by Your truth,
And that Your truth will remain
Forever in me, always in my inner being.

What Are My Doors?

What are my doors?
The doors that allow the enemy free entrance,
To come in and seduce me,
With his lies and devices of trickery?

What are the doors that I unfasten and let fail me,
Even with full knowledge that the enemy awaits to destroy me,
To confuse and cloud my mind,
To make this open door or that open door seem okay?

What doors do I tear down on my own
In my rush to gratify flesh?
Do I willingly unleash the turbulence that jeopardizes my walk
To appease what I want and what I see?

Radio. Television. Books. People.
A few of the names, the categories for the doors
That I must gain discernment over,
To quickly judge whether it is a door to be closed,
To close as quickly as the door I open, when
Jesus knocks to come sup with me.

Worship in Restoration

He has restored the beauty from the ashes.
He has given me vision; I see the victory.
He has released me and freed me.
I see happiness and joy and peace again.

I see hope and joy in my days.
I see the hope and future of His provision.
It is not a mystery, and it is no longer hidden from me.

I dance in praises to Him,
Lifting my hands and twirling in the rays of His love.
I dance in my mind when I can't physically express it.
I leap in joy, and He leaps with me.
He holds my hands and we dance, directing
My steps and making them sure.
It's beautiful; it's artistic, art in motion.

It is love taking flight and soaring,
With more being received from what is released.
This is a worship waltz,
A worship in restoration,
Ushered in praise
And made perfect by the Holy One,
Showing up and directing, orchestrating, and leading the steps.

> To appoint unto them that mourn in Zion, to give unto them beauty for ashes, the oil of joy for mourning, the garment of praise for the spirit of heaviness; that they might be called trees of righteousness, the planting of the LORD, that he might be glorified. (Isa. 61:3 KJV)

You Ain't No Friend of Mine

You ain't no friend of mine,
Standing up in my face, perpetrating a fraud.
Whispering things in my ear purportedly for my good.
Cleverly hidden misdirection that teeters little by little closer to the edge.

You ain't no friend of mine,
Scheming and plotting to get me off course.
Smiling with lips, yet the smile doesn't quite meet your eyes
As your tongue whips back and forth, hot air gushing
Past flashy pearly whites, quickly presenting lies.

You ain't no friend of mine,
Gathering around me, throwing thoughts and ideas,
Overcrowding my senses,
Taking me away from my plans, His goals, my purpose.

You smile, you flatter, your lips sing praises to me, feeding me
A stomach full of deceit, until I can't stomach it anymore.

Because your words have reached
A part of me that immediately disassociates with it,
Causing an unrest in my spirit that though I wandered away,
Transfixed by the glitter of your fancy dust,
My spirit did a double take.

As you pressed your luck and your plans
Past that realm,
That invisible line that says, whoa, that's way too much,

So just jump back before I sit you back.
Because I know what I know.
And even though my mind may have slipped into believing you,
I will not fall, nor will I walk or sit or stand in your midst.

Get out of my face, thou king of deceivers.
Jump back and stay there.
You ain't no friend of mine.

Quest for Perfection

I'd like to be perfect in Your eyes.
I get sad when I can't attain it.
When I stumble and mess up,
When I make excuses or give up,
I feel sad way down in my soul.

I know You give us a will to choose,
And I know the ways that I have strayed.
But in times when my choices traded good for bad,
I wish for Your will and that
My choices were Yours and not mine.

These times I wish You'd just make all my ways straight,
Take away my options, so I can't do any wrong.
I think, *If You'd just take away the things in me that are wrong,*
Then I'd always be perfect in thy sight.

But You desire for me to make the choice.
Out of Your love for me, You've given me a free will.
You've also given me a manual
To guide me to victory.

It is Your love that desires love in return,
For us to make choices out of love also.
And in that love, and in my quest for perfection,
I know that it is impossible to reach without You.

I'll try my best to do my best,
To align my walk with Your Word.
My quest for perfection is not for my glory
But to bring glory and honor to You,
So that one day, of me You will say, "Well done,"
As You embrace me in the perfection of You.

She Waits at the Gates—Flee the Temptress

Prelude
There is a place that you often travel, although you know you shouldn't.
You travel those old familiar roads, even though
You end up in the same, dry, dead place.
Why is it that when you know that the end of *that* stretch of
Tarmac will produce only emptiness, desolation, and tears,
Why do you still turn your mind away from the known end
In order to live in forgetfulness today?

Why do you offer up a blind eye to those places you shouldn't venture
But a deaf ear to clear instruction, God's instruction?
Why do you trade His guidance for the reasoning in your mind,
The reasoning that justifies your intentions and
Makes them right, at least in your own eyes?
At least long enough for you to pursue them?

You see the reasoning and roads traveled,
Which provide a temporary escape
From the things in life that one doesn't want to face,
They often disguise a sly seductress,
Who stands at the gates of the city, offering words to derail our path.

Those words sound sweet.
The presentation looks so nice,
And the invisible arm draws you ever so near.
Don't be misled by her winks or the ease of her smile;
She dances a dance with scarves laced with lies.

These scarves tangle and swirl all around you,
Motioning, beckoning.
A cloud of pinks, violets, yellows in the finest silks,
While she moves in a dance that hypnotizes
And causes you to forget.
You're soon too caught up to notice your extremities are bound.
You're soon wrapped up in it.

She caused you to forget that you saw her
standing at the gates in times past,
When she lured you with her wares, and you were trapped in her snares.
And once trapped, she takes great pleasure in leading you astray.
Once trapped, you see that all her beauty and her promises
Are as ashes that the wind doth blow away.

Resist her as she urges you, as she pleads with you to lie in her bosom.
For the pleasure she promises are but death to your progress,
And her bosom's goal is to smother life completely.

Chasing a Feeling

Chasing a feeling, in need of healing.
To break away from the unseen grasp,
Snared by the very thing that your flesh seeks.
From an addiction you feel you can't release,
A dance with steps drawn out from the past.

Chasing a feeling, in need of healing.
To overcome the plague on your life,
Attached onto you from generations past.
Following your lineage to trap you in the very same prison
Even now, even unto you.

A feeling can be so temporary, so fleeting.
One feeling seems to help as you transcend its highs.
But when the winds of the feeling die down
And the moment is gone,
The original feeling is back, beckoning strongly, even stronger.
And you are left alone in the emptiness of—a feeling.

All alone with the original feeling,
The feeling that you tried so hard to replace.
Whether it's a need for love or acceptance or confirmation.
Or maybe to relieve fears, doubts, or insecurities.

Perhaps its loneliness, lack of fulfillment, frustration.
Maybe the need for attention, affection, or just understanding.
Whatever name to call this feeling, this feeling
That drives the need for your healing,
Beyond the temptations that leads to a temporary release.

Don't fill in the hole left by a feeling
With empty, temporary vices by chasing yet another feeling.
Those feelings don't lead to your healing.
Those emotions can have a limited shelf life.

Replace the feelings with the Word of God.
His Word holds His promises for you.
Replace the feelings in His presence
As you chase Him in praise and worship of Him.

His Word combats negative emotions and feelings.
And it is in His Word where the healing is wrought.
Love above all love
Even in the midst of His suffering.

Beauty for ashes,
Joy for mourning,
Hope and an expected end.
Grace for the new day.
Favor and mercy.
He will never forsake you.
He is always your friend.

Guidance, a path directed,
The vices lost quickly, deflected.
No condemnation, but all things working for good,
All needs supplied
By the One who died
On the cross
As a payment for the lost, a payment for our sins.

A perfect love to cast out fear,
Strength through Christ's sufficiency.
Peace that was left for you, for me.
An abundance of weapons to defeat those feelings,
Feelings that the tempter has beaten you down with.

Replace that feeling with God's love.
Replace it with His Word, cling to His promises.
No matter how rough your situation seems,
Stand firm in your obedience to God's instructions.

If you have fallen, get back up and receive forgiveness.
Don't let the feelings bind you; don't let the feelings condemn you.
Your release is in the fact that Jesus has died and arose for you,
For you to have a release from a feeling,
A feeling that goes against His loving plans for you.
Be free from a feeling; receive His healing.
He has already left it for you.
He loves you.

Honor, Thanks, Appreciation, and Worship

Praise Break!

A Beacon for God

Many search long and hard
For someone such as you.
Someone who gives unselfishly,
Never expecting a return.

Always lending a helping hand,
An attentive ear, a strong shoulder, a strong back.
Heavily laden and pressed with
Burdens that are not directly yours.

Giving of your time
When there's hardly any to spare,
Encouraging, uplifting, promoting.
You are always willing to share.

A magnet to those searching
For help that's hard to find.
A lighthouse in a wretched storm
That guides the forlorn wanderers safely home.

And even when the thunderous praise
Is sung in thanks for all you do,
You do not take the credit.
You say God works through you.

It is an honor and a privilege
Just to be in your presence.
Because where you are,
Jesus is also,
Beaconing, warming, sheltering, and blessing.

Intermission of Thanksgiving and Praise

Thank You, God!
Praise extended to You!
Broadcast, sound blast,
A major force of praise!
A catapult, rushing waters of my praise,
Trajectory speed defying sound barriers,
I give, I lift-up praise to You.

Intimacy of the Walk

More of You to complete me
As You inhabit my being.
More of Your true, love-filled whisperings,
The song that I dance to,
The cadence of my walk.

My fibers lie in anticipation,
Sensations enlightened to the acknowledgment of Your presence.
My fibers rejoice in the intensity of the touch of Your love
As You shower Your love through me.

The intimacy of Your aura,
It alone gives cause to my joy.
This peace and satisfaction deep within me,
It reflects upon the strength I gain in Your arms.

I look unto the hills of my help,
My answer to all that I need.
This intimate walk in Your love
I desire, and there is no place I'd rather be.

Just to Say Thanks

Lord, I thank You.
You continue to pour into me,
Even past my failures and frailties,
My perceived or realized stumblings,
You give unto me.
You love me.
You see me.

Linked

I want to be linked so tightly with You that one could not tell where I end and You begin; The me who I once was becoming indecipherable against the me that I am becoming in You.

I want the me that I have been in the past to die down forever so that my rebirthed spirit, with my renewed mind, is known as the true me, and it is the one that You do see.

I want my recreated spirit to reflect Christ so clearly that my transformed spirit is seen before my humanly attributes can be accounted.

I want the fruit of Your Spirit to be so evident in me that the tree that my fruit falls from can only be traced back to You. After all, as the saying goes, a tree is known by its fruit.

I want my seed to bear the seed of Christ to perpetuate Your holy garden.

Intermission of Thanksgiving and Praise 2

Even now, I feel that it is so crazy how much I love writing.
It is so awe-inspiring how much peace and happiness writing brings to me.
I feel as though I'm sharing with God some of my thoughts and heartfelt wonderings. What makes me tearful sometimes is also the feeling that in writing, God is also answering!
Hallelujah!
Praise be to God, my Father!

Worship with My Pen

I worship You with the stroke of my pen
As it relays Your Word
From the spring of Your everlasting fountain.
The outpouring of the living water
That flows so freely as an offering,
A tribute to sacrifice given.

They pierced You in the side.
And out from You poured blood and water, the source of my living water.

I worship You with my pen.
Use me as You alone see fit.
Fill me and qualify my hands
To wrap themselves around the words that are captured in my heart.

I worship You with my pen,
Offering up a praise using the gift that You gave.
I give a gift back as an offering.
I extend to You Your rightful glory, the
Worship, praise, and admiration due.

Never trying to diminish or supplant Your gift,
The gift that has revealed new levels of dreams to me.

Anointing flow.
God, let Your blessing smear my dreams with Your power,
This vessel to become everything You purposed it to be.

Pour out Your Spirit.
In the last days it is to flow.
Pour out Your Word.
Pour it forth from my heart, from Your revelation, from Your inspiration.
Anoint the work of my hands, the stroke of my
Pen as I use it in worship of You.

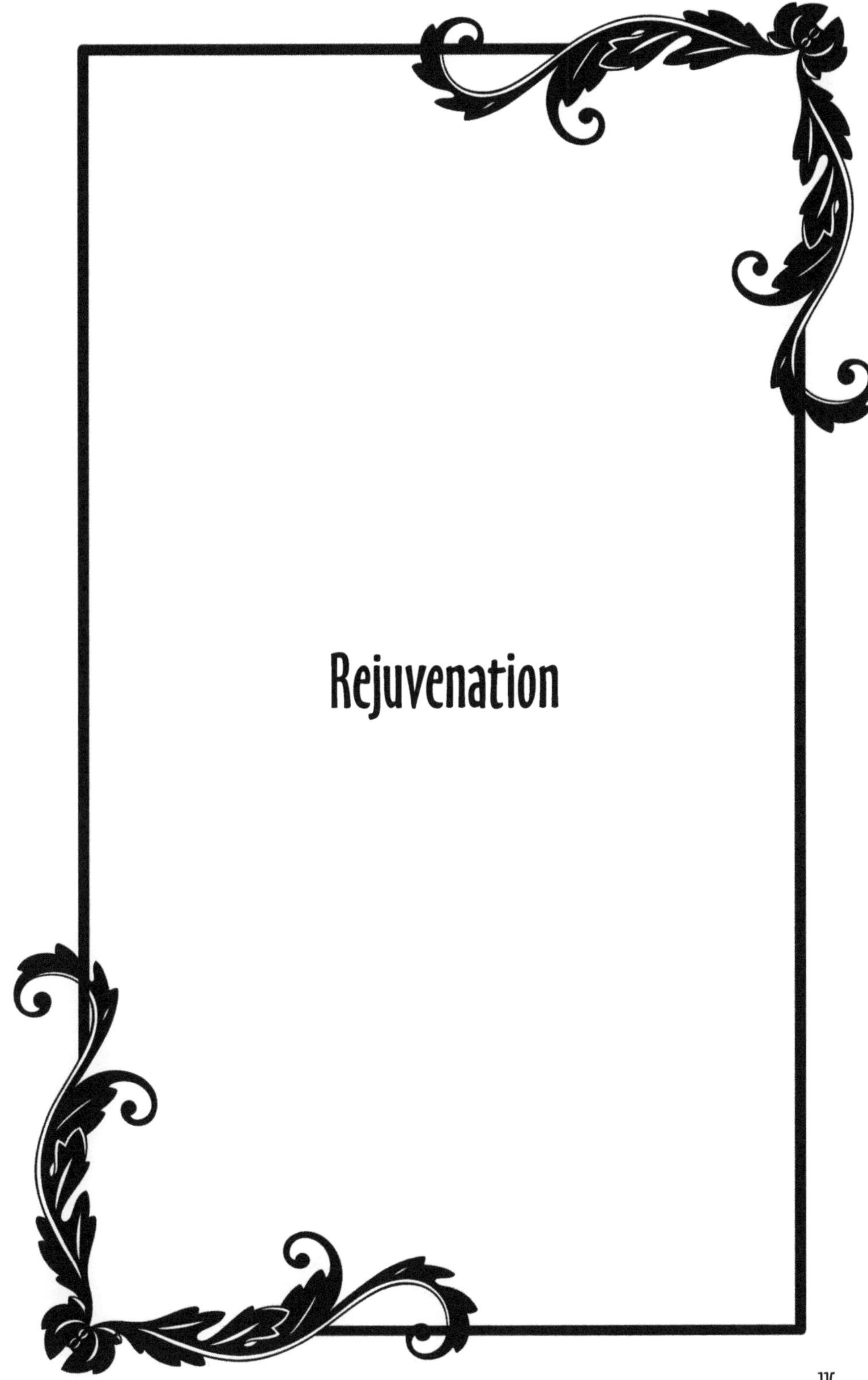

Rejuvenation

Breath of Life

Breathe life.
Let it flow freely.
Swirling over, in, and among crevices,
Reaching inside the innermost parts.
Breathe life, oh, breath of life.

Breathe life into every situation—
Long buried, encrusted in dirt, and settled.
Cast into the sea of Oblivion, of forgetfulness.
Revive to Your purposeful state.

Breathe life into the dust, yielding new formation.
Oh, breath of life, breathe life.

A cool, savory aroma
Encapsulated in peace and hope,
Changing the unchangeable by mere will.
Breathe life, oh, breath of life,
Giving of Your life-saving power.

Flow freely, unhindered, and unchecked.
Reign and cleanse.
Purge and pursue.
Breathe life, breath of life, as manna of deliverance.

Increase My Measure

Increase my measure.
Increase my faith.
New levels I see before me.
I sense it past the natural.
It's too good to be from me.
A preparation for what You know is to come.

Increase my measure,
Increase my faith
To knock down any hindrances to break through.
The silos of Your promises are widened, overflowing.
Let not doubt or unbelief narrow their capacity for release.

Increase my measure.
Increase my faith.
I won't let pride get in the way.
I know I need what I ask of You.
I know You hear this, my earnest and thirsty prayer.

Deliverance from an illness that
Can't possibly be held onto.
An illness wrapped so tightly of fear, of reservation, and doubt,
Cloaked and almost hidden in unbelief.
I rejoice that the diagnosis has been revealed.
The Physician is now free to heal.

To increase in me
The measure of faith,
To build upon that that was originally granted
As I spell out and demonstrate in countless ways
The very truth of the source of this need.

Faith to move the mountains
Though steep, rugged, unyielding, and covered in snow.
Faith to activate Your Word

And to walk in boldness with the confidence from You.
Faith to be me in all the splendor and uniqueness of how You made me.
Faith to just trust in Your wisdom and Your love.

Faith that can't be stagnant.
Although by a mustard seed portion, You can perform miracles.
If by grace of a mustard seed faith,
What more faith when my seed continuously grows.

Increase my measure.
Increase my faith.
I long to grow in You.
Diligently I seek
For the Rewarder to bequeath
A stronger reinforcement to my shield,
To strengthen my arm as I valiantly hold up and wield
This, my shield of faith.

As I grow and grow in faith,
Using the source of the Word as my fertilizer,
My expectation is for the shield to get heavier
As it gets infused with much-greater faith.

I get more rooted and steadfast in faith.
You, Lord, provide increase and the grace
With all provision made for me to carry it,
My much-improved shield of faith.

See, I was told I am more than a conqueror.
By faith, I must believe it's true.
That is fertilizer, causing my seed to grow.

See, I was told that my God would make
All things work together for my good.
I believe, and I receive it.
That's causing my seed to grow.

And then I was told
That whatever I ask for when I pray,
That if I believe it and I receive it and it is in line with Your will,
Then it's mine.
And that is more fertilizer, causing my seed to grow.

I was also told that I could do all things
Through Christ's sufficiency.
I choose to believe it,
And it's causing my seed to grow.

And then I was shown that
He loves me—
Evidenced by His sacrifice, His grace, and His mercy—
And told that His love never fails.
I believe all that I've seen,
And it's causing my seed to grow.

See, I have a miracle grower
That I spread on my seed,
And it works like nothing I've ever known.
It's truly a wonder
How much greater my measure
When I nourish it with His Word speaking to me.

His Word is the root, the source of my food,
The teller of that good news
Heard with spiritual ears.
It is the real,
The authentic fertilizer,
Which nourishes me and causes my seed to grow.

Mind-Changing

Mind-changing,
Blocking the inlays imprinted and fashioned,
Carved into the crevices,
Into the inner workings of my mind.

Mind-changing,
Forcefully denouncing the words spoken.
Emblazing my mind in an attempt to fill, to override
What He placed there,
Trying to destroy, and in its stead,
To fill the void with—lies.

Mind-changing,
Willing and working toward,
Not allowing empty and wasted spaces, vacant lots,
To take up residence in my mind
By filling it up with You and Your Word.

Mind-changing,
Mind altered, focused on You.
Your thoughts become mine.
Your words imprinted on the facets of my mind,
> Newspaper print,
> Monospaced font,
> Glossy or embossed graphics,
> Headlined,
> Saved, stored, and
> Backed up—daily.

Mind-changing.
Warfare fought and won.
Source the mental plains.
Destination, an altered mind and heart,
Steady state, ready state,
Steadfast and transfixed on Your Word.

Your Word that brings peace
To guard my mind, my heart.
Mind changed, altered forever
By Your transforming power.

Focus

Drop That Zero

It's time to drop this acquaintance.
She's been hanging around for years.
She only shows up when I have big things to do.
She comes and takes over while I am unaware.

Although I remember her clearly.
We were road dogs back in the day.
Whenever I needed to blow off some steam,
This little homie would come running my way.

We'd drop from one scene to the next scene.
She and I would head to nowhere fast.
This long-lost associate of current times,
Who knows just when to make an appearance in my life.

She was there when I needed to spend time with You.
She convinced me of ways to better occupy that time.
She convinced me to whittle away the minutes with her,
And before I knew it, I said for You, "Maybe next time."

She popped in when I first saw the vision.
I saw the great things that You laid out for me.
You revealed a dynamic future.
You showed me a world of ways to make it come to be.

She came through just to holla, and I chose to hang out with her.
All the commitment, the ideas, the intentions were soon forgotten.
She has a knack of making waste to my plans.
She ramrods right through, and my goals just went for naught.

She is there, this associate who seems to have an insight
Into what's going on in my nights and my days.
How does she know the things I long to do?
I think back, and I am yet amazed to realize

That this acquaintance has kept me off course.
She has delayed me in every step I tried to make.
Each and every time I have a chance to advance,
This ole girl just gets in the way.

It's time to drop this acquaintance,
This associate, this fair-weather friend.
She has a plan to delay and derail me
From my God-promised purpose and my expected end.
She is a leach of my time and my energies.
She's shadowed by laziness, her best friend.
This once so-called associate is procrastination.
But alas, this association has met an abrupt end!

Inspiration text:
> This book of the law shall not depart out of thy mouth; but thou
> shalt meditate therein day and night, that thou mayest observe
> to do according to all that is written therein: for then thou shalt
> make thy way prosperous, and then thou shalt have good success.
> (Josh. 1:8 KJV)

Lest He Come Suddenly

I will not be found sleeping.
Nor will I be found slipping.
I stand firm to keep watch,
Vigilant in my post as the Master commandeth.

To each is given a job, a duty, an assignment,
Given by One having great authority and power.
Detailed steps are a part of His holy instruction.
He's been very thorough, not leaving anything out.

A work to be done; few committed to do it.
Nevertheless, the task is yours to complete.
You are accountable to the job description given to you.
Whether you do it or not is your choice.

Don't be lazy and unfazed by the requirements of the day.
Press hard to stay on task.
Maintain tunnel-like vision, and remain focused on your assignments.
Make a concentrated effort to strive ahead.

We know not when the Master returneth.
So let Him not return to find you sleeping.
Step aside, and impose a watch on yourself
Lest He comes quite suddenly and of your
Assigned work you have nothing to show.

And as you work, help, and encourage others
So that each job in the Master's plan will be achieved,
In unity, let us all work together,
Working hard to make each goal come to pass.

As for me, I will not be found sleeping.
Nor will I be found slipping.
I stand firm to keep watch,
Diligent in my post as my Master commandeth.

No Authority

I am not an authority.
I never professed to be.
All I know, all I can attest to
Is how great God's been to me.

He's been a great lifeline,
My comfort in knowing I am not alone.
Holy Spirit leads me,
Giving me confidence in what is said in His Word.

Sometimes we seek this title,
This confirmation, this "You are the best."
But why seek it in earthly places?
I'd rather hear my Father say, "Well done!"

No, I am no authority.
Can't even claim to be the best.
I just endeavor in what my Father has given me,
And I let Him take care of the rest.

I listen and absorb in worship and praise,
And let His words take lead of my heart.

I am, after all, only His servant,
Trying to make my Master proud,
Pushing forward in what He's given me
One instruction at a time.

Not all in the right ways.
Not all my i's dotted to rule.
But I will not be dissuaded.
I still have my job to do.

No more comparisons.
No more timid-filled delays.
I want to be the best
Instrument of me that only I can be.

So that as God uses me,
And I faithfully walk out into unknowns,
God is filling me with grace,
Giving me the power, authority, and credentials
Needed to get the job done.

Working in me as I press forward in purpose
So that one day I can hear God say,
"Well done, my beloved daughter.
I love you, and I welcome you home."

No, I am no authority—not alone, not by myself.
I don't have all the credits, degrees, or the seals.
I just endeavor in what my Father has gifted unto me.
He makes my work complete.

As I listen to His instruction,
As I offer up praise and worship to Him,
I let His Word take lead of my heart
As I study and follow Holy Spirit.

I probably won't always do things your way
Even though it may have better appeal.
See, I have to trust in what my Lord says.
In His name and by His power, my authority is made complete.

Sam

A memory that's fleeting yet persistent,
So dependable.
A foundation set so strongly of love,
So undeniable,
In your own ways showing.

A glimpse here, a flash-point video speeding
Across the forefront of my mind,
Bringing with it a smile.
To know such comfort,
So comforting.

I recognize and recall the gentleness of your care.
Your dreams for me, your speaking life to me and over me
So becoming,
Enabling me to become.

A good man leaves an inheritance to his
Children's children.
Your words, thoughts, and teaching
In the short time we knew each other
So uplifting,
So empowering,
So treasured.
What an inheritance!

I wonder at the heights of achievement
The crossroads I could've overcome with you at my side,
So steadily encouraging.
Nonetheless, the foundation was set, and so
I break through each level
So prepared,
Taught to expect to excel.

Jesus, You placed people in my life to light my path,
To bring forth the things I need,
Whether love, support, or care.
You set people in motion to ensure my way was prepared.

You went back in time
Through to the record of my birth,
To the point where purpose was defined,
To appoint me to become an ambassador in this strange land.
Yet You prepared me to fulfill that purpose
Before I even existed here on earth.

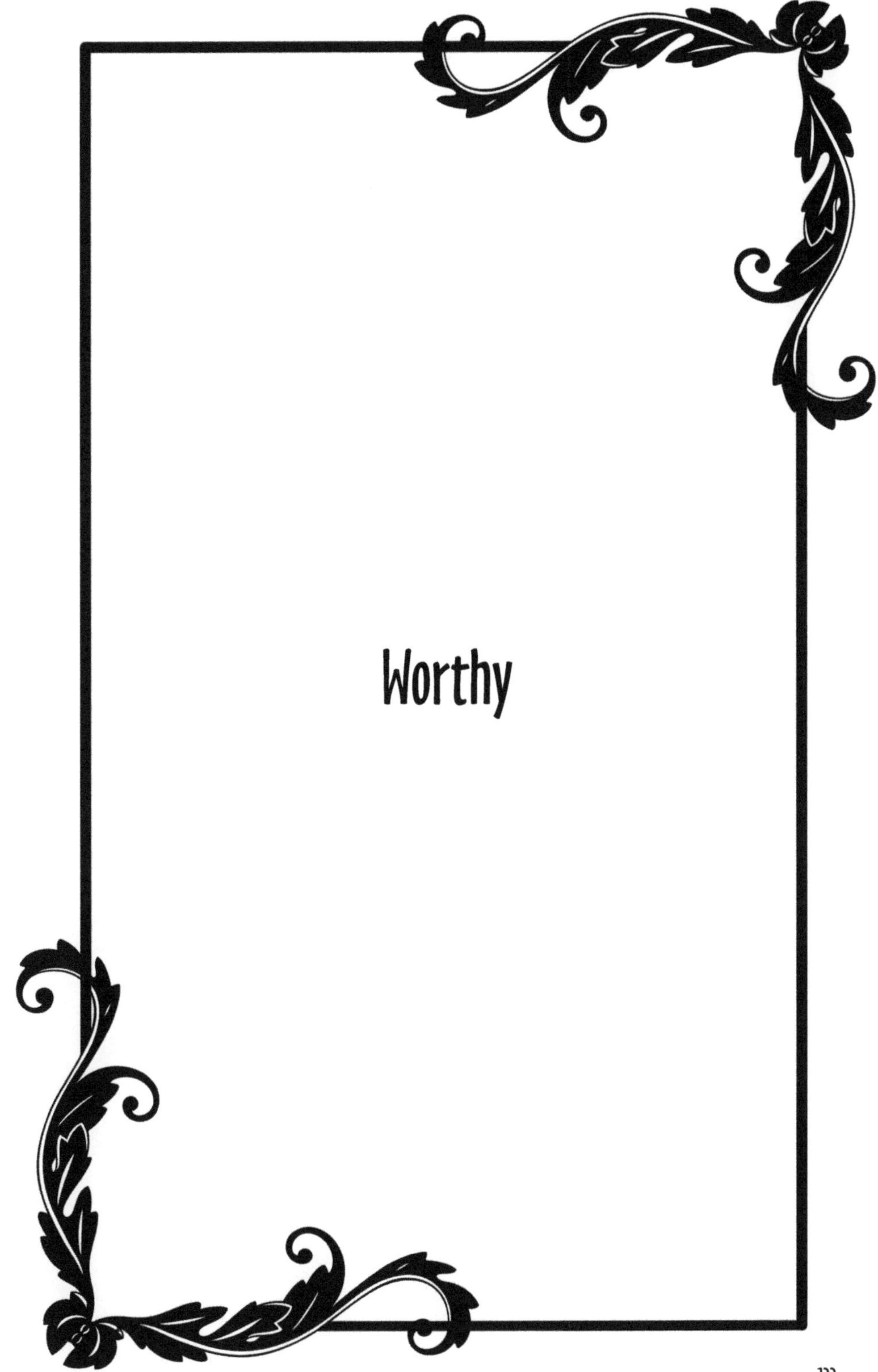

Worthy

Different

You've always been a li'l bit different.
(I made you that way.)
Thought a li'l different,
Dreamed a li'l different,
Saw things a li'l different.

Not learned.
No examples.
No one to show you the way.
No one to show you *this* way
To make you *that* way.

Just the opposite.
Everything to show otherwise.
Yet you are different.
Rejoice in different.
You are worthy!

Who Am I?

Who am I to oblige
The things you say about me,
To enter into your proclamation
Of whom I am destined to be?

Who am I to entertain
The imaginations you set for me,
To assist in the captivity you bring
When Jesus died to set me free?

Who am I to discount
The evidence of a supreme love,
To seek the very thing God gives freely
From a calculating and uncaring world?

Who am I to deny the power that God has set aside for me,
To deny my own potential
And to not live in power faithfully?

Who am I to listen to the lies that you and your crew whisper to me,
To believe I am any less magnificent
Than the person God designed me to be?

Who am I to desire admiration and respect from you,
When you dispel any hopes I've ever had of growth and remaining strong?

Who am I to look to you
As my example of what's fun, acceptable, and true,
When everything you give comes with a price,
The knowledge of which you are extremely careful to hide?

I am tired of your lies and your perpetrating as my friend,
When all you really desire is to steal,
To bring my hope, my peace, and joy to an end.

You want to leave me destitute,
Downtrodden, isolated, defeated, and lost.
To seek fun in your ways of doing things
And to not recognize the cost.

But I know deep down within me
That following you would be seeking in vain.
What I need would be forever elusive.
In a viscous circle, likened to forty years in a desert, I'd remain.

If I try your ways,
Maybe I'll find fleeting relief
For the need I just can't define.
But after a season with you on my side,
I feel more needy and in a state of constant decline.

Who am I? Let me tell you
Just a little bit about me.
I am one whose blinders have come off
And who walks boldly toward victory.

I am one with new eyes,
And I now see what secrets lie beneath
Your cunning planning and devious ways
That kept me in defeat—past tense.

I am more than a conqueror
Through God, whose Holy Spirit resides in me.
So you haters must take heed.
My mind is renewed, changed, and set free.

I am the seed of my Father,
Who has formed and fashioned all of my days,
Who has carefully carved my future
Out of the lovingly, crafted plans He has laid.

How long I had dwelled there,
How many times I failed,
Those things don't matter anymore to me.
You see, I have boldly stepped out of my wilderness.
And by faith, His grace, and mercy,
I am finally free!

Why Me?

Why me?
When my heart just can't get right,
When I too quickly give up the fight,
Trembling, in unbelief, I walk on my path.

Why me?
When I try to shut out the light,
Hidden in darkness, is Your glory to be denied
Because I feel it can't be in me; I am not worthy?

Why me?
You could choose from the entire world.
The cream of the crop that floats to the top.
You see it all clearly; You have insight to see all,
To see all the best,
To see who is better than the rest.
To see all who are better than me.

Yet You point Your finger.
You set Your focus on someone like me.

Why me?
I don't understand it.
Perhaps if for a moment You would shed some light
Over my plight,
Then maybe I could see what You see in me.

And I ask again, "Why me?"
I don't deserve it.
I am too frail to meet it.
The benchmark is much too high.

Why me?
Don't You know where I come from?
Don't You know what I've been through?
Can't You see the pain that I try to hide?

Why me?
I try to deny it,
Yet You keep calling,
And I feel You even more and more.
I try to drown out the sound of Your voice,
But it is still You, and I know it.
It's still You that I heard
When I asked, "Why me?"

And You let me know that it is just because it *is* me,
That You love me in all Your truth,
And that love never fails,
That loves never goes astray
Even if I do.

Your grace is sufficient.
Your grace stamps out condemnation,
So I don't have to suffer in this walk.
Because I am walking continually toward You,
Because I continue to hear from You
Even when I fear what I hear You calling me to do.

Why me?
Your love shines on me.
It embraces and engulfs me.
It turns me around in its embrace.
Your glory can't be replaced.

A vessel with cracks,
You chose like its precious.
Oh, so precious to You.
Why me?

Too Much

You are
Too fat; you're too skinny.
Too uneducated, just too intelligent, you know-it-all.
Or at least you *think* you know too much!
You are way, way too ghetto, too stuck-up.
You come from a broken home; your parents always fought.
You don't even know your dad; your dad is all you know.
You grew up poor; you grew up with money to spare.
But with parents who never cared; they were never there.
You do not enunciate properly; you are too country, too Geechee.
You are too timid; you are too popular, too popular for that or for them.

You grew up in the projects; your family owns
Multiple houses and much land.
You are too introverted; your bubbly personality
Works everyone's last nerve.
You are too generous, must be showing off.
You are too stingy, too friendly, too solitary,
Too angry, too forgiving, too weak.
You are just
Too. Too. Too. You are *too much*.

Words whispered, lies told, temptations presented.
An automatic replay.
Images broadcast in high definition
Of the lies as they unfold.
Over and over.
Over and over.
Over and over they play.
Yet in actuality,

You are
Too much.
Too much of everything in you.
But still you cry, "It's not enough."

Too much…not worthy?
Too much…not capable?

Do you see the contrast?

When God says
You are beautiful, created in His image,
You have too much in you.
I Am is in you.

You are more than enough because God overfills your cup,
Granting you an abundance of too much
Of everything you need, of the gifts He wants you to receive.
So whose definition of "too much" do you believe?
Who do you follow?
Whose voice do you heed?

God loves you enough to have sent His Son to die for you.
Jesus died for you because God loves you too much.
God has given you too much if only you will see it, if
Only you will believe it, if only you will receive it.
Yes, God has given you too much.
 Too much to sit silently,
  Listening to lies from someone who has seen a glimpse
   Of how much, how too much
   God has placed into you.
   Of the too much that makes
   You more than capable.
   Of the too much—blessings
   Just waiting in store for you.
   Of the too much in God's adoption of us
   You inherit worthy.
  Listening to the lies from someone who is jealous
   Of how much God loves you,
   Of how much God favors you,

Of how much God values you,
Of how much God wants you; God wants you!
Because even the enemy knows the truth
In that
God will always love you too much!

You Define Me

You define me.
I was created in Your likeness.
You breathed Yourself into me,
Molding me in Your completeness.

You submitted Yourself,
Bled and died for me.
Covered me in the helm of Your salvation,
Redefining my destiny.

Changing the course of my future
To overcome death and have victory now and in my eternal life.

You define me.
You made me an heir, joint heir with Jesus,
Giving me great authority and a great destiny.
Your love bestowing power and position to me.

You created a new covenant,
Shedding the one of old.
Jesus the ransomed, sacrificed,
A much greater sacrifice than those of old.

See My Eyes

See my eyes as they shine before You,
A collage of different scenes.
And traipse beyond the boundaries
Of what image Your mind receives.

How Your Light Shines

Your light beams forward
Whether you realize it or not.
It surrounds your countenance,
Painting a picture for the world to see.

The picture shows clearly.
It can't be masked.
Even if no one addresses you,
They remember what's seen, although not always said.

Lonely Little Girl

Lonely little girl
In a world she doesn't identify with,
Looking at it
While in it,
But above it, if you will.
Looking on it, if you will.
Like, "No! No!" to the sad little image.
Yet lonely,
Not knowing fully that she's not alone.
No, never alone.
The "not-enough" feeling burgeoning inside her
Befriended this lonely one,
Pursued this lonely one,
Distracted this lonely one.
By whispers of friendship,
By the acceptance of longed-for quick acceptance,
Whispers introduced, befriended, petitioned, and persisting
Distracted this lonely one.
Lonely little girl,
The "not-enough" feeling burgeoning inside her.

Purpose

A Journey

A journey,
A journey past a particular mind-set
Engraved with a pen long ago.
When did it happen? Who knows?
I certainly don't, and I never saw it coming.
What causes me to feel less or incapable?
Why do I sometimes feel like my best isn't good enough,
Even if others say I've exceeded their expectations?
Often, my silent, inner question, posed to them in secret is,
"Then what, exactly, were your expectations?"
Imagining that they didn't think I could do it anyway,
As a means to keep the mantle of my not being good enough, anyway.
Because if they knew what I know in my mind,
The fact that, that was okay, still isn't good enough.

Why isn't it good enough? Why isn't my best good enough for me?
Why can't I see what others see or accept a compliment?
Is it because I don't think I'm good enough,
that I don't think I am worthy?

A journey.
I look back, and I am seeing a picture of me that I've never longed to see.
I am realizing that I am not the self-assured
Person I've been pretending to be.
A lack of fulfillment has taken a grasp onto me,
And I realize it is because whatever I do does not
Seem good enough—if only to me.

Why isn't it good enough? What am I measuring myself against?
Is it too impossible that I can't achieve it?
My journey starts anew
With the realization that a gift given to me can't be escaped.
I never feel good enough because I know that a part of me

Fears the purpose living in me; I was created for it, yet I fear
That the realization of it will make others see or think
She's not quite good enough.

But in this journey, I have now come to really embrace a release,
A release in that it is okay for me to not be good
Enough in my own feeble hands.
But in God's hands, I stand corrected.
In God's hands, my frailties are consumed in His ability.
His love consumes me and provides the lift,
The assurance, the, "You can do it,"
To bolster me past my biggest hindrance, me.

My journey is not based on what I can do or what lies beneath
The wonderings of a mind that was fed by an enemy.
My journey is not walked alone and is not
Based on how perfect I am in myself.
But it is strengthened by God's love perfecting
Whatever He has called me to do.
My journey has begun anew.

Let Me Be Perfect for You, Through You

"Let me be perfect for You, through You."
"I got you."
"My strength is made perfect through your weakness."

You try and try, and yet it doesn't seem enough.
Not quite right.
Not there yet.
Working and working,
Striving to do your best.
Giving your all.

You heard the vision.
It was made plain.
You grasped, held, and clung to it.
You ran with the vision,
But there appears no change.

No change in your circumstances, yet it seems to have gotten worse.
You went over a mountain, prayed through a valley,
Yet you seem to be at the same place.
You work harder,
You take on more,
Study more,
Listen more,
Achieve more.
And yet the circle remains.

You believe the Word.
You proclaim abundance in your life.
You long for God's joy, His good life, His promises.
You see what appears to be a manifestation of it in others.
You try what they do to get there,
Yet you still have a lid on.
You are still boxed in.

You want to run, run into what you know God has for you.
You want to scream, scream to bring it down,
To bring it to pass and to shatter the glass walls that surround you.
Walls that still bind you, yet you can see where you are supposed to be.
You can see what God has for you.
You can see your good life, your abundant life, your joy.
These glass walls still have a lid on it.
You can see the blessings.
Blessings to rain down, but they can't meet their mark.
It's because of this lid that your works can't lift.

A circle, in walls, with a lid on it.
What a mess!
What frustration!
What imprisonment!
What else can you do?

"Let me be perfect through you, for you."
The Lord wants you to step away from your works,
And step away from trying to get "it" through your own might,
Might you let God work for you?
Shoulder the load?
Put His power on you to shatter the glass of your glass walls
And to remove the lid so that your blessings rain down on you?

Let His strength lift you over that mountain
And usher you through the valleys,
Your works.
You ran with the vision; let Him run with you.
God, giving your feet flight like hind's feet,
Allowing you to run straight into your victory,
Straight into His promises,
Straight into the vision of the life and plan that He has for you.

He runs and flies and soars with you.
And as you run into your abundance, your joy, and your peace
With arms outstretched, He embraces you
As He laughingly enjoys your stepping into His joy,
And releasing Him to perfect the path, the road,
The travel, the experiences, the flight.

Let It Flow

Let it flow, let it flow.
Let Your anointing flow.
I feel the power that has been infused into me.
With knowledge comes release to unleash the potential
That I now know has been birthed into me.

A supernatural rendering of power,
I sling it like Spiderman's web.
The discovery of its potential
Has spelled new life and meaning into me.

I now walk in greater confidence,
Not of me, but of Christ's strength in me.
I have a new outlook on the future, a new boldness and assuredness.
Another weapon securing His path laid for me.

Use this, your orifice, to let purpose flow.
Let it flow, let it flow, let it flow.
Holy Spirit, guide this lump of clay
With Your power as a breath of life poured into me.

What's Really, Really Real?

What's really, really, real
When confusion is all I feel
As I struggle to try to step out into
The life my mind reveals?

What's really, really, real
Above the unrest within my soul
As I cry out in earnest supplication
My requests to be made known?

"Is there something missing?"
Is my utmost cry.
To search and never find it,
Is my quest to be denied?

Real above the fictitiousness,
Above the fakeness of the world's show.
I escape above the artificially portrayed view
To find the meaning that I long to know.

What's really, really, real
When the blinders are all taken off
As I fight generations of aimless wandering,
Of walking out the motions but still being lost?

Real being more than examining
The concrete aspects of a thing,
But to examine the very essence of what's there,
Although abstract to the naked eye.

Why be tossed among the waves of emptiness
When there's life all around?
Is it selfishness that steals joy
When peace seems nowhere to be found?

What's really, really, real?
Faith, does it all lie within you,
The substance of things hoped for,
The evidence of things not seen?

Is real defined by having
Faith in what I know above mere feeling
Past emotions, beyond carefulness and fear
To the purpose that lies beneath, marking me as being real?
My answer to the quest for realness revealed
Even as I seek it for myself.
What's really, really real I found in continuously seeking
My God and living out His holy will.

My unrest is due to unrealized, unfulfilled purpose.
It keeps me feeling empty, like I've missed the mark
To fulfill God's divine plan for me,
The level of real meaning in my life.
I desire it with all my heart.

Now that the definition is clear
And confusion is forever bound,
What's really, really, real is not a question to ask
Because in God's will is where the answer is found.

> Now faith is the substance of things hoped for, the evidence of
> things not seen. (Hebrews 11:1 KJV)

Word Beating

The colors of my imagination are vivid to behold.
They race in a kaleidoscope of colors that the rainbows pause to admire.
Stronger than the stroke of a key, my mind weaves fascinating tales.
Books come alive in three-dimensional views as
My eyes glide among their pages.
The words become one with my mind, melding the
Words and experiences to my thoughts.
I paint those very same words on the sketch-
Board of my mind with agility and ease.
I draw comfort from the written word.
There is an affinity there, a sense of being in sync.
It's like meeting someone you've always known;
A friend you've longed to see, but never met.
Death and life are in the power of the tongue, but the output
Of the tongue comes from the formation of words.
Words from the heart to the tongue have authority and power.
My responsibility is to let them flow, to breathe,
Garner, and encourage life via words.
I am required to let them flow, but temper
Them with love and compassion.
God is my guide.
For He is the Word, and the Word is He; the Word is my guide.
I let God guide my words; the master artist gives new
Imprints to my mind to make even old words renew.
Hmm. God, please continue to renew my mind with Your Word
As I hungrily feast on Your Word.
Yes, I feast on Your Word from the beginning, in the now,
And even transcending time; yes, even my time.

Excited

I am excited about the plans You have for me.
Your will for my life does not lie in mystery.
I hear Your voice.
I lie in wait, not anxiously, but eagerly
Because I know that You have great directions for me.

You pour out to me the things for each new day
That cause me to align more and more with Your will.
I listen, being careful not to strain my ear for each new
Word, visual, or idea that You would impart onto me.

I am excited.
Lord, I know that You have plans for me to prosper,
To have the enjoyable life of Your original intent.
Your heart's desire is that I live each day to its fullest
And that I reach my fullest potential.
You desire that I have a smile as my constant
companion for I am enamored with You and the
blueprint that You have fashioned for my Life.
Just for me.

Lord, my excitement grows as I glean new ideas and know that
Through Christ, I have the ability to make them come to pass.
I have great strength through You.
You have metamorphosed me into this new being,
This ever-changing being who lives to praise and worship
You in song, in deeds, and in the work of my hands.
I take joy in Your choice of a vessel.

I am excited.
I try not to let my excitement cloud my hearing.
I know that the result of the masterpiece
That You've created in me is great.
I have strong desire to get there,
But I also know that in the journey, each seemingly little step

Offers a brilliance of its own that I am careful not to miss.
You see in the excitement of the journey, I want to pick
Up every token of wisdom, creativity, laughter, hope,
Love, and enjoyment that each step brings.
I am excited, Lord, and that excitement is all about You!

Fresh and New

New and uncharted territory,
Fresh as the morning dew,
Crisp and clean and refreshing,
Reenergizing a state that's been burned.

Meadows alive with new beginnings.
A yearling starts out on its new voyage,
Traipsing among the dew-dotted, spring flowers.
Fresh hope for a brand-new dawn.

It looks forward to the new day ahead
Enjoying the fresh, cool morning,
Scanning the horizon filled with endless possibilities,
Embracing peace as it eagerly moves along.

How awesome is that feeling?
To look forward to each new day
Carrying God's peace, joy, and calmness all around you,
Flowing on the wings of His grace
With the purpose He originally designed.

Time

Time ticks on.
It cares not who is dependent on it.
It has yet to wait on anyone.
Instead, it hastens to do its job.

Time does not sit still.
I wonder at its tenacity.
As I look back in retrospect, I often wonder
Just where all the time that I thought I had has gone.

Time to do the things I've always wanted.
To spend with family and friends.
Time to absorb the best of every moment,
To enjoy every second given.

I fully realize something that I always had a form of knowledge of:
That time carries on without ceasing its plan.
And I must do the same, forging ahead with my plans
And governing my time accordingly.

So take time for the things that are important.
Read that book to the kids.
Take your mom on that trip.
Because in the twinkling of your eye,
The time you thought you had
May become just a mere image of what was left unsaid and undone.

Life in Abundance

I want to live life richly
On multiple levels.
A rich life is promised to me
If I seek, trust, love, and fully obey Him.

I want the over-the-rim, cup runneth over life in abundance,
Never doubting, fearing, or worrying
About satanic hindrances or stumbling blocks before me.

Where everyday's experience is
More fulfilling than the last.
And as I reflect on days past,
I can only smile, exhale in remembrance of it, or laugh.

I want each second of each day
To count in living out my purpose.
In any area of ministry afforded me,
I can expect grace and look forward to it.

I want to transcend the rat race
And the world's view of the way things should be.
I want to enjoy life in abundance.
It is God's will for me.

As I thank God for each new day,
The grace and mercy reserved especially for me,
I want to see the majesty of it all
As His favor shines down on me.

I want to dissect the elements of time
That encapsulate and try to pose barriers around me.
Dissect it so thoroughly that its mandate
Hold no limits for me.

Of all the abundance granted through my days,
I can play from my memory's recordings
To encourage, to witness, to truly say
I have lived the abundant life by God's grace.

> He shall pour the water out of his buckets, and his seed shall be in many waters, and his king shall be higher than Agag, and his kingdom shall be exalted. (Num. 24:7 KJV)

> Blessed shalt thou be in the city, and blessed shalt thou be in the field. (Deut. 28:3 KJV)

> Blessed shalt thou be when thou comest in, and blessed shalt thou be when thou goest out. (Deut. 28:6 KJV)

> Behold, I will bring it health and cure, and I will cure them, and will reveal unto them the abundance of peace and truth. (Jer. 33:6 KJV)

> For if by one man's offence death reigned by one; much more they which receive abundance of grace and of the gift of righteousness shall reign in life by one, Jesus Christ. (Rom. 5:17 KJV)

> Mercy unto you, and peace, and love, be multiplied. (Jude 1:2 KJV)

Greater Work

There is a greater work that is in me.
It is suppressed and must be released.
The fire of the anointing infuses me
With His power, so I must succeed.

This work is not for my edification.
It's an obligation to birth help for someone else.
My body is the orifice for power
That flows from an unending, unyielding Source.

As each challenge comes forth,
I will trust in my Source,
And let the power for each new level perform its work
By faith and relationship with the greater One who is in me,
The author of my greater work.

It Is Not about Me

Holy Spirit,
Please help me in this walk.
Whenever I feel like I'm there, that I've arrived,
Gently remind me to be humble,
To not deny that I have this flesh
That wars against any achievements, my
Purpose, and any potential progress.

Let me see that the end of the line moves,
So there is no true finish line.
But You have provided the power to aid me
Through each lap, each hurdle, each height to ascend.
You have given me the power to propel me forward
To cross new finish lines, to achieve new victories.

If I get weak, You have the necessary ingredients to reenergize me.
If I get tired or bored, You have the creativity to inspire me
And lead me to new paths and new ways to accomplish the same tasks.
To win each new race.

There are no mundane, monotonous routines in You,
Not when my walk is done for You,
And my walk is not for me,
Or for any form of self-acknowledgment, or self-importance.
You are my greatest cheerleader, my biggest fan, my coach,
Showing me all the training, all the plays, to achieve new victories
And to accomplish each task in excellence,
In integrity, and in completeness.

So if I get "in myself" to the point where I think *I* did it,
Or that my walk, my setbacks, or my achievements are all about me,
Guide me to the knowledge of my original purpose, in who I do it for.

Acknowledgments

A special thanks to my parents and to my parents gifted through marriage. I thank you for your love, provision, protection, support, guidance, talks, and encouragement. Thanks for pouring into me in varied stages. I thank God for gifting me you, and I love you.

To my siblings, my cousins who are like siblings, and my siblings whom I have chosen, you know this book has been well over ten years in the making. Thank you for your years of encouragement and for still believing in me, even when all I could say is, "It's coming soon." The bond we share is priceless. I love you all.

To Apostle Sam and Lady Annette of Abiding Word Family Ministries (AWFM), thank you for sharing God's Word, undoctored and with simplicity of understanding. Thank you for your leadership, for your example, your prayers, for your love and support. Thank you for helping lift me up in some of my toughest moments and celebrating my happiest ones. I love you, appreciate you, and thank God for you! Thanks also to the AWFM family. You have aided my growth in many ways, and I thank you.

To my friends and extended family, thank you for your encouragement, friendship, and fellowship. Thank you for listening to me—some for decades—talk about writing, and then about this book in particular and "walking out" my purpose. Thank you to my accountability partners, who consistently remind me of purpose. Thank you for letting God use you to highlight purpose and for being steadfast accountability partners. You all have been invaluable.

To everyone who has offered an encouraging word, read a poem in advance, or offered advice, I thank you. To everyone who will read this book, I thank you, and I hope it blesses you!

Lightning Source UK Ltd.
Milton Keynes UK
UKHW010651260220
359364UK00001B/62